4 95
2 95

# THE SOCIAL DANCES OF THE
# NINETEENTH CENTURY IN ENGLAND

# THE SOCIAL DANCES
## OF THE
# NINETEENTH CENTURY
## IN ENGLAND

*By*

PHILIP J. S. RICHARDSON

*President, Official Board of Ballroom Dancing*
*Vice-President, Royal Academy of Dancing*

LONDON : HERBERT JENKINS

*First published by*
*Herbert Jenkins Ltd.*
*3 Duke of York Street,*
*London, S.W.*1
1960

PRINTED IN GREAT BRITAIN
BY CHARLES BIRCHALL & SONS, LTD.,
LIVERPOOL AND LONDON

# FOREWORD
by
## VICTOR SILVESTER

IT is with pleasure that I write this short foreword to Philip Richardson's latest book on dancing. I suppose that P.J.S. (as he is affectionately known) might well be described as the "doyen" of the dancing profession, but probably few people outside the dancing world can even imagine the valuable and lasting contributions that he has made to it.

I first met Mr. Richardson in 1919 when I was competing in my first-ever dancing competition in Ostend, and he was one of the panel of judges. After the competition was over I was presented to him, a tall and erect man with a greying moustache, who topped my own six feet by several inches. His quiet and unassuming charm immediately put me at ease, and this was the beginning of a long and continued friendship which has lasted to the present day.

P.J.S. has been associated with almost every branch of dancing, but as I know him so well in connection with ball-room dancing, I can best refer to what he has done in this field alone.

In the early 'twenties ballroom dancing was in a chaotic state, as there were no laid-down rules for any teacher to follow, and what you would learn at one school would in no way resemble what you would learn at another. It was Philip

Richardson who suggested to the Secretary of the Imperial Society of Teachers of Dancing that a committee should be formed to sort out the tangle of dancing steps then being taught and to lay down a standardisation of dances. A committee of six dancing teachers was formed in 1924, and I was one of them. From the basic work done by that Committee has come the English style of ballroom dancing that we know to-day, and which has been copied by almost every country in the world. But if Philip Richardson had not had the foresight and shrewdness to suggest what he did, I often wonder how many years would have passed in chaos, and whether ballroom dancing would have existed in its present form.

For over forty years Philip was the editor of a paper which he had started in 1910. This magazine became the voice of dancing, and in 1956 it was divided into two separate monthly publications, *The Dancing Times* and *The Ballroom Dancing Times*. Philip voluntarily retired as editor a few years ago, but he still remains as President of the Official Board of Ballroom Dancing, a body of representatives from the main societies. Similar to the Lawn Tennis Association or the Football League, the Official Board lays down the rules by which our profession is governed. One man was responsible for the setting-up of this body, and he is Philip J. S. Richardson, O.B.E., who has devoted his life to the betterment of all branches of dancing.

To-day at eighty-five P.J.S. is still young. He has always moved with the times, and any advice he offers carries the weight and authority of long experience. When you read this book you will realise that this is the work of an expert with a greater knowledge of dancing history than any other man alive to-day.

## ACKNOWLEDGMENTS

In a book of this nature it has, of course, been necessary to include many quotations from by-gone writers and all these have been acknowledged when used. There are in addition a number of my friends to whom I should like to give my thanks for the help they have rendered.

I am grateful to Mr. George Begley, then of Dublin, who gave up a number of hours to search the files of the old papers in connection with the Countess of Farnham's famous ball in 1817; to my friend Douglas Kennedy, O.B.E., Director of The English Folk Dance and Song Society, for kindly reading the chapter on the Country Dance; and to Ivor Guest who, with some difficulty, secured for me the picture of the Redoutensaal in Vienna. I also want to thank my colleague, Miss Mary Clarke of *The Dancing Times*, for valuable help, suggestions and advice.

To Miss Valerie Prentis of the Royal Academy of Dancing (Teachers Training Course) I am indebted for much useful information on the subject of women's dress during the nineteenth century, and I am equally indebted to Mr. W. T. K. Braunholtz of The Institute of Gas Engineers, for putting me in touch with Mr. E. G. Stewart, a retired member of that Institute, who sent me some very interesting details of the gas lighting of dance halls.

7

In America I am very greatly indebted to Miss Lillian Moore for the many researches she made on my behalf. I also want to give my grateful thanks to Mr. Arthur Murray for permission to quote somewhat extensively from the delightful publication *Down Memory Lane* written for him by Sylvia Dannett and Frank Rachel.

Finally I want to thank my publishers, Messrs. Herbert Jenkins Ltd. who, on seeing the first draft of this book, made certain suggestions which necessitated its being re-modelled. Although these alterations did not appeal to me very much at the time, I am now convinced that they were absolutely right.

P.J.S.R.

# CONTENTS

9

# LIST OF ILLUSTRATIONS

# THE SOCIAL DANCES OF THE
# NINETEENTH CENTURY IN ENGLAND

## ★ I ★

## INTRODUCTORY

THIS book is an attempt to tell the story of those social dances
which found favour in England during the nineteenth century, that is from 1801 to 1900. I shall endeavour to describe
how they originated, trace their development during the
century under discussion and, if they are no longer danced,
find some logical reason for their disuse. At the same time
an effort will be made to correlate these happenings with the
social life of the time.

It is obvious that the dances in vogue at the very beginning
of the century must have a history stretching back into the
eighteenth and possibly even into the seventeenth century
and earlier. In order therefore to present as true a picture as
possible of the years 1801 to 1900 and not to cause any confusion in the minds of my readers, anything that happened
to a dance prior to 1801 is given in a preliminary part of this
volume which, in the fashion of accountants, might be called
"Brought Forward".

I have included also in this preliminary part some account
of the places where they danced, notably the old Assembly
Rooms. Here again it has been necessary to delve deep into

15

the previous century because the characteristics of these Rooms were formed long before 1801.

In the case of certain important dances of the nineteenth century in which dancers of to-day, notably old time dancers, still show some interest, I have extracted from contemporary writers a technical description of the original steps. While of great interest to the teacher and the historian I realize that such descriptions might weary the ordinary reader and so I have placed them apart at the end of this book.

It will help towards a clearer understanding of the Ballroom dancing of any particular period, if it be remembered that this form of dancing is primarily a social pastime and is, of a consequence, influenced by changes in our social life during or preceding that period. It must never be regarded as something apart from the rest of the world, existing by itself in an hermetically sealed compartment, impervious to what is happening outside, for as the habits and the customs of the world change, so will our social dancing.

As a rule the reason for an alteration in our dancing is clear. For example, the tremendous social upheaval caused by the French Revolution and the shattering results of the two world wars were bound to leave indelible marks on our social life and, therefore, on our social dancing.

These changes have always been going on. As long ago as the beginning of the thirteenth century, the dispersal of the Troubadours of Provence through the Courts of Europe, following the slaughter of the Albigensian Crusade, spread the idea of the "couple" dance. This they had evolved, as a result of their ideology, from the more impersonal Carole and Farandole and thereby exercised a great influence on the future of the Dance.

In 1520 we had the pageantry of the "Field of the Cloth of

VAUXHALL GARDENS
From an old engraving of 1754

RANELAGH

A view of the Canal, Chinese Building, Rotunda, etc., during a Masquerade

Gold" at Guines in the Pas-de-Calais when Francis I entertained King Henry VIII, and probably many of the English Nobles saw for the first time the basses dances which were then in fashion at the French Court. Anyhow, it must be something more than a mere coincidence that the very first printed description in English of these dances was published in 1521 when John Copland added to a French grammar a treatise describing *The Manner to dance Bace Dances*. The only copy of this work is in the Bodleian Library, Oxford, but it was reprinted with explanatory remarks by Mr. John Guthrie, The Pear Tree Press in Bognor Regis, in 1937.

Sometimes the original cause which has led to a change in our dances is so widely separated in time from its effect that the association of the two events is not at once obvious. For instance, the transfer of thousands of African Negroes to the three Americas by the slave traders two hundred years ago brought to the New World those primitive African rhythms which, amalgamating with those of the British, French, Portuguese and Spanish settlers, yielded the so-called Latin American dances of to-day.

The great national movement which towards 1840 swept those European countries then under alien governments helped to draw the attention of Western Europe to such dances as the Polka and the Mazurka, but the changes caused by the gradual rise of the Bourgeoisie in the second half of the eighteenth century, by the romantic revival in Literature at the beginning of the nineteenth century and by the industrial revolution during the century were more subtle.

As a curious example of cause and effect, it has been said that the existence of Prohibition for many years in the States, by sending thousands of thirsty pleasure-seekers cruising to the West Indies, put New York society in touch with the rhythms of the South, and so expedited the arrival of such dances as the Rumba in the ballrooms of the world.

A careful study of the history of our social dances during the past two or three hundred years reveals the fact that a new dance, if it is to have a world-wide appeal, must come from a folk dance. Even the courtly Minuet traces its origin to a folk dance of Poitou, and the all-conquering waltz to a turning dance of German peasants. It is the coming of a new rhythm that is important; the original steps are not of such great consequence and these frequently change as the dance is developed for the ballroom. Indeed, if a dance does not develop and undergo changes, it will stagnate and die.

I have also noted that, at any rate in the past and before the coming of the present jet and radio age, in the country of its birth the successful new dance was a social climber.

It started with the common people and gradually ascended the social scale until it was accepted by the aristocracy. In other countries which adopted the dance the reverse process has taken place. It was the travelled aristocracy who introduced the dance to their ballrooms in the first instance and the more popular assemblies which slowly learned to copy the prevailing fashion. We have seen this in our own times. The Foxtrot sprang from the darkies of North America, and it was some time before it was accepted in the best ballrooms of New York. From here travelled Americans and English took it across the Atlantic to the smart ballrooms of London whence it permeated downwards until it reached the more popular assemblies.

It would be as well for readers to bear in mind that in the nineteenth century—particularly during the first quarter—class distinctions were very strongly marked and exercised a great influence on our social life and consequently on our social dances. Even at the close of the century there was a wide difference between the programmes favoured by the upper classes and those in vogue at popular assemblies. For this reason I have thought it advisable to give (Chap. II) a brief account of some of the old Assemblies both immediately prior to and during the century we are studying. This class distinction held good until after the first world war, and the opening of the modern Palais de Dance.

Some readers may urge when they have read the following pages that, although this purports to be a history of social dancing in England, I have devoted quite a lot of space to what happened in Paris. This is because Paris was for so many years the hub of the social world of Europe, and what happened in Paris was copied in other countries. As a result, very many of our dances came to us via the French capital.

The nineteenth century was one of particular interest to students of our social dances because it witnessed the beginning of our modern dancing. It marks the great change from the "open couple" dance of the eighteenth century, as exemplified in the Minuet, and the coming of the modern "closed couple" dance as shewn in the waltz.

There is a saying "History repeats itself". It is rather a hackneyed expression, but it is very true as regards dancing. It will be found that a knowledge of what has happened in the past in somewhat similar circumstances will form a good guide to the possibilities of the future. As Lord Byron once wrote "The best of Prophet of the future is the Past".

## ★ 2 ★

## THE ASSEMBLY ROOMS PRIOR TO
## THE NINETEENTH CENTURY

BEFORE considering the dances which found favour in England during the nineteenth century, it will be as well to say a few words about some of the places where they were danced—places which will be mentioned from time to time in the following pages—and in particular about the old Assembly Rooms.

The earliest Assembly Rooms were possibly those at Hampstead, Tunbridge, Epsom and Bath, all places, it will be noted, associated with medicinal waters, and of these by far the most famous were those at Bath.

The apparently strange connection between Assembly Rooms and places associated with invalids in search of health has been well explained by Oliver Goldsmith in his *Life of Nash.*

"A spirit of gaming had been introduced in the licentious age of Charles II and had by this time thriven surprisingly. Yet all its devastations were confined to London alone. To this great mart of every folly, sharpers from every country daily arrived for the winter, but were obliged to leave the Kingdom at the approach of summer in order to open a new campaign at Aix, Spaw,

or the Hague. Bath, Tunbridge, Scarborough, and other places
of the same kind, were then frequented only by such as really
went for relief; the pleasures they afforded were merely rural,
rustic and vulgar. In this situation of things, people of fashion
had no agreeable summer retreat from the town, and usually
spent that season amidst a solitude of country squires, parsons'
wives, and visiting tenants, or farmers; they wanted some place
where they might have each other's company, and win each
other's money, as they had done during the winter in town.

To a person, who does not thus calmly trace things to their
source, nothing will appear more strange, than how the healthy
could ever consent to follow the sick to those places of spleen,
and live with those, whose disorders are ever apt to excite a
gloom in the spectator. The truth is, the gaming table was
properly the salutary font, to which such numbers flocked."

The curative value of the Hampstead waters had been
known since the days of Charles II, but it was not until the
beginning of the eighteenth century that a serious attempt
to popularize them was made. Social attractions were added,
including the building of an Assembly Room known as the
Great Room in Well Walk. Two thirds of this was used as a
ballroom and the remainder as a Pump Room. For a time the
venture was a success and Society flocked to Hampstead
Wells, but soon the card-playing and dicing attracted a
rougher element and Society stayed away. In 1733 the Great
Room was converted into an Episcopal Chapel. Later on, when
a new assembly room known as the Long Room was built, the
glories of Hampstead were to some extent revived. The vir-
tues of the waters were re-discovered and Society returned.
Goldsmith, Fielding and Smollett were to be seen there and
literature of the late eighteenth century contains many
allusions to the wells. Richardson's Clarissa Harlow had a
long-drawn-out adventure at Hampstead and Miss Burney's

Evelina paid a memorable visit to the Rooms when Mr. Smith danced his famous minuet with Madame Duval.

It was at Bath that Beau Nash, the most celebrated of all Masters of Ceremony, reigned supreme as a veritable King of Bath. His amusing but extremely autocratic Rules for the conduct of the Assemblies became the model for all other such Rooms.

He went to Bath as Master of Ceremonies in 1705 and shortly afterwards drew up that extraordinary set of rules which regulated not only the conduct of frequenters of the Assemblies but the general behaviour of the visitor to the City. Amongst these may be quoted the following:

"That no gentleman give his ticket for the Balls, to any but gentlewomen.—N.B. Unless he has none of his acquaintance."

"That gentlemen crowding before the ladies at the ball, shew ill manners; and that none do so for the future, —— except such as respect nobody but themselves."

"That the elder ladies and children be content with a second bench at the ball, as being past or not come to perfection."

The balls held on Tuesdays and Wednesdays were by his direction to begin at six and end at eleven precisely, nor would he suffer them to continue a moment longer, lest invalids might commit irregularities, to counteract the benefit of the waters.

Each ball was to open with a minuet danced by two persons of the highest distinction present. The lady then retired to her seat and Mr. Nash brought the gentleman a new partner. This ceremony was to be observed by every succeeding couple, every gentleman being obliged to dance with two ladies till the minuets, which generally lasted two hours, were over. At eight the country dances were to begin, ladies of quality, according to their rank, standing up first. At nine came a short interval for rest and tea. Country dances were then resumed until the clock struck eleven when, even if in the middle of a dance, the ball terminated.

Beau Nash and his methods had many imitators, and no more ardent one than the despotic Miss Nicky Murray at the first and extremely exclusive assemblies held in Bells' Wynd, Edinburgh.

With the passing of the Gambling Law of 1745 which deprived Nash to a considerable extent of his sources of income his popularity began to wane, and this combined with his rudeness and the inevitable approach of old age drove him from the city. He passed the last ten years of his life in straightened circumstances, but on his death in 1762 he was given a magnificent funeral by the citizens of Bath.

Four years after Nash's death the orchestra in the Assembly Rooms was led by a young Hanoverian whose knowledge of music was gained from a short experience in the band of the Duke of Cumberland's army from which he had deserted. The young man who remained at Bath from 1766-1782 spent all his spare moments constructing, with the help of his sister, telescopes. He was none other than William (afterwards Sir William) Herschel, and with one of these telescopes in March 1781 he announced to the world the discovery of the planet Uranus. Ultimately he became Astronomer Royal.

During the second half of the eighteenth century a number of extremely sumptuous Assembly Rooms were opened in the heart of fashionable London doubtless to cater for those who did not wish to make the journey to Vauxhall or Ranelagh. These were Carlisle House in Soho Square (1763), Almack's in King Street, St. James's (1765), the Pantheon in Oxford Street (1772), and the Argyll Rooms in Regent Street. Of these the most important and indeed the only one which really interests us in our study of the nineteenth century was Almack's.

These rooms were built by William Almack, said to be a Scotsman from Galloway whose real name was MacCall, with the profits he had made from the launching of one or two West End clubs—notably that originally known as Almacks Club, but subsequently as "Brooks". He first came to London when in the service of the Duke of Hamilton, and subsequently married the Duchess's waiting maid. The premises were opened in February 1765, and in spite of extremely inclement weather and the unfinished condition of some of the rooms, the occasion was honoured by the presence of the Duke of Cumberland and a number of distinguished visitors. Horace Walpole in a letter to the Earl of Hertford under date February the 14th, 1765, wrote:

"The new Assembly Room at Almack's was opened the night before last, and they say is very magnificent, but it was empty; half the town is ill with colds, and many were afraid to go, as the house is scarcely built yet. Almack advertised that it was built with hot bricks and boiling water—think what a rage there must be for public places, if this notice, instead of terrifying, could draw anybody thither. They tell me the ceilings were dropping with wet, but can you believe me, when I assure you the Duke of Cumberland was there?—Nay he had a levee in the morning, and went to the Opera before the Assembly! There is a vast flight of steps, and he was forced to rest two or three times. If he dies of it,—and how should he not?—it will sound very silly when Hercules or Theseus ask him what he died of, to reply 'I caught my death on a damp staircase at a new club-room'."

The ballroom was a magnificent chamber considerably larger than the corresponding room in Carlisle House. From the start there was always a certain exclusiveness about Almack's, but it was not until the beginning of the nineteenth century that it attained that degree of exclusiveness for which it had become famous. An advertisement in the Daily Press four years after it had opened ran as follows:

> On Friday next, the 10th Instant, at ALMACK'S Assembly Room in King Street St. James's, will be the First of the two Nights Subscription for Minuets and Cotillons, or French Country Dances. The Doors will be open at Eight. No Person admitted without their Name wrote on the Back of the Ticket.

In 1772 the arrangements for the coming Winter Season are set out in another advertisement:

> ALMACK begs Leave to acquaint The Nobility and Gentry, Subscribers to The ASSEMBLY in King-Street. That the First Meeting will be on Thursday the 17th of December Inst. for the ensuing season.
>
> There are to be in the twelve Balls four Mask'd Balls, which the Subscribers have for the same Subscription as usual. For each of those Nights there will be 200 extra Tickets issued out, which can be had only by the Order of one of the Ladies that hold Books, at Two Guineas and a Half each Ticket.
>
> 'Tis most humbly requested of the Gentlemen in particular to send for their Tickets in Time, as positively no Person whatever can be admitted without a Ticket, nor any Tickets delivered out upon the Ball-Day.

Concerts, for which there was a further subscription list, were also held at Almack's, and for a time its rooms were used by an extremely exclusive ladies' club from which there probably sprang that Committee of great ladies who governed its destiny at the turn of the century, when a ticket for one of the balls at Almack's was one of the most difficult things in the world to obtain. Of the three hundred officers of the Foot Guards, it is said that only six ever obtained admission.

On two occasions the great Duke of Wellington was refused admission. Once because he arrived after midnight, and once because he was wearing trousers instead of knee-breeches.

Although they were closed some years before the beginning of the nineteenth century mention must be made of the notorious Mrs. Cornelys and her assembly at Carlisle House, as this place will be referred to later on. Carlisle House stood in Soho Square on the site now occupied by St. Patrick's Church at the corner of the modern Sutton Row. It became celebrated for its famous masquerades which were attended by all the "smart set" of the day. Madame Cornelys was continually getting into trouble with the authorities and the rooms were ultimately closed.

The Pantheon, which was opened on the South side of Oxford Street in 1770, was the scene of many remarkable masquerades during the closing years of the eighteenth and the first few years of the nineteenth centuries. It was a truly magnificent building and writing at the time Horace Walpole said:

> "The new winter Ranelagh in the Oxford Road is nearly finished. It amazed me myself. Imagine Balbec in all its glory. The pillars are of artificial giallo antico. The ceilings even of the passages are of the most beautiful stuccos in the best taste of grotesque. The ceilings of the ballrooms and the panels are painted like Raphael's loggias in the Vatican; a dome like the Pantheon glazed. It is to cost fifty thousand pounds."

In 1789 its Grand Salon was converted into a theatre which could temporarily take the place of the burnt out King's Theatre. Ballet-goers will remember that the Sadlers Wells production *The Prospect Before Us,* named after the picture by Rowlandson is based on the change over from one theatre to another.

In 1792 the Pantheon itself was destroyed by fire, but it was rebuilt and once again became the scene of many big masquerades including a masqued ball in honour of Lord Nelson in 1791. It then became in turn a Ball Room, Bazaar, Picture Gallery and finally the offices of well known wine agents.

The Argyll Rooms in Regent Street were opened by Colonel Greville under a committee to rival the Pantheon. They soon became fashionable. They must not be confused with the New Argyll Rooms opened later on the site of the present Trocadero Restaurant as a popular assembly. The rooms in Regent Street were rebuilt in 1818, but were destroyed by fire in 1830, on which occasion for the first time the steam fire engine was used.

By the end of the eighteenth century the vogue for open air pleasure gardens had passed away. Of the more important of the seventy pleasure gardens in the London area the famous Marylebone Gardens, referred to in "The Beggars Opera" and frequented by Pepys, Handel, Dr. Arne and Dr. Johnson, had closed down in 1763. Bagnigge Wells in Clerkenwell with its once fashionable Long Room, though lasting well into the nineteenth century, had fallen on evil days and lost its smart reputation. Only Vauxhall, the parent of them all, and Ranelagh survived. These "Pleasure Gardens" bore some resemblance to the similar Gardens opened in Battersea Park in connection with the Festival of Britain of 1951, and in a lesser degree to those at the White City and Earl's Court of over a generation ago. Dancing facilities were provided, but these formed but one of many attractions. Of Vauxhall Gardens which were on the Surrey side of the river, and generally approached from fashionable London by water, Horace Walpole wrote after visiting the rival Ranelagh Gardens on their opening night: "I was there last night but did not find the joy of it. Vauxhall is a little better, for the garden is pleasanter and one goes by water." Later on, however, he changed his mind and said: "Every night constantly I go to Ranelagh which has totally beat Vauxhall. Nobody goes anywhere else—everybody goes there. My Lord Chesterfield is so fond of it that he says he has ordered all his letters to be directed thither." Even in its palmy days Vauxhall seems to have been a risky place for a young lady to walk in unattended, as Evelina in Fanny Burney's novel found to her cost. In its latter days not very reputable Bals Masqués were held which caused a lot of annoyance to the neighbouring residents. The Gardens were finally closed in 1859.

Ranelagh Gardens were on the north side of the river close to the present Chelsea Hospital, and boasted an enormous Rotunda. Its circumference was 555 feet and the internal diameter 150 feet. In the Grand Tier there were fifty-two boxes in which suppers were served and also further boxes in the Gallery. In 1802 Boodle's Club gave an immense Ball here, and on June the 1st, 1803, there was another great Ball given by "The Knights of the Bath". The gardens closed about 1805.

It is possible that the fashionables of the day found it irksome making the long journey to Vauxhall or Ranelagh and being somewhat at the mercy of the weather, and so the opening of Carlisle House in Soho Square and Almack's in King Street, St. James's, in 1763 and 1765 respectively, already referred to, undoubtedly played a big part in deciding the fate of the Pleasure Gardens.

It is true that there was a large platform at Cremorne Gardens in Chelsea which were opened in 1830 and flourished on popular lines for about thirty years.

# ★ 3 ★

## THE ASSEMBLY ROOMS
## DURING THE NINETEENTH CENTURY

SOME of the Assembly Rooms tended, particularly towards the beginning of the nineteenth century, to become extremely exclusive and local tradesmen and all "theatricals" were forbidden entrance. For example, at the Assembly Rooms in Cheltenham, which were opened by the Duke of Wellington in 1816, the year after Waterloo, amongst the rules governing admission appeared the following:

> "That no clerk, hired or otherwise, in this town or neighbourhood; no person concerned in retail trade, no theatrical or other public performers by profession be admitted."

At the beginning of the nineteenth century the old procedure was still maintained at Bath. The rules governing admission to these Assemblies were as stringent as ever in theory, but a lower degree of exclusiveness was beginning to creep in. The minuet was still danced and followed by the Country Dances which were probably a little more sedate than those seen at popular affairs. No Master of Ceremonies since the death of Nash had the personality or the power of that autocrat. Jane Austen in *Persuasion* (published posthumously in 1818) wrote:

The Theatre and the Rooms were not fashionable enough for the Elliots, whose evening amusements were solely in the elegant stupidity of private parties.

The Victoria Art Gallery and Municipal Library at Bath have a collection of letters written by Sarah Webb whose portrait painted by William Payne is in these rooms. In one of these dated April 17th, 1822, she says:

> Bath had been pretty full lately but upon the whole it has been rather a thin season—there used to be three public Balls a week and this winter there has only been one but there is so many Private Balls and great Routs I believe is the cause.

Charles Dickens sent Mr. Pickwick to Bath in 1828 and gives a fanciful and possibly highly exaggerated picture of Angelo Cyrus Bantam Esq., the then Master of the Ceremonies, who might possibly be identified with Lieutenant-Colonel Jervoise who actually occupied that office from 1825-1849. At night at the Assembly

> "he wore a brighter blue coat, with a white silk lining, black tights, black silk stockings, and pumps, and a white waistcoat, and was, if possible, just a thought more scented."

Even at this date every effort was apparently made to keep up the exclusiveness of these Assemblies, as the following quotation also from the Pickwick Papers, shows:

> "The Ball nights in Bath are moments snatched from Paradise, rendered bewitching by music, beauty, elegance, fashion, etiquette, and—and—above all by the absence of tradespeople, who are quite inconsistent with Paradise, and who have an amalgamation of themselves at the Guildhall every fortnight, which is, to say the least, remarkable."

During the first half of the nineteenth century the dances in fashion at Almack's were copied everywhere and, as we shall see later, it was in these rooms that the Quadrille and the modern Waltz were introduced into England. Almack had died in 1781 and the control of the rooms passed to a Mr. Willis who had married a niece. Later they became known as Willis's Rooms, and still later in the century Willis's Restaurant was a favoured dining-place. This passed away and a firm of auctioneers occupied the premises until they were severely damaged in the Second World War.

From a contemporary guide of the period I extract the following details of a typical Assembly Rooms, namely those at Margate, at one time regarded as one of the finest in the country.

These, opened in June, 1769, stood at the South corner of Cecil Square and formed a very handsome building with an imposing frontage of Doric columns. In front were the grand suite of apartments including a coffee room, several convenient rooms, with a commodious billiards room, etc. On the first floor were the tea and card rooms and the ballroom, the last named being a very fine room eighty-seven feet long and forty-three feet broad.

The season commenced each year on the King's Birthday and closed with the last ball night in October. There were generally about 1,000 subscribers. The fees payable may prove of interest:

"That every person to be entitled to walk and play at cards in the rooms during the season do subscribe Ten Shillings and Sixpence and none but the Subscribers be admitted into the card room, except on Ball Nights.

"That on Thursdays (Ball Nights) Subscribers do pay one shilling and sixpence admittance and non-subscribers four shillings.

"That on Sundays Subscribers do pay one shilling and non-subscribers one shilling and sixpence."

The cost of cards will doubtless interest modern bridge players.

The rule stated :

> "That all persons playing at whist, quadrille, commerce or loo, do pay eleven shillings for two packs of cards and seven shillings for a single pack. No other games to be played without the permission of the Master of the Ceremonies."

At these rooms about 1830, when Captain Clough was Master of the Ceremonies, most stringent rules were in force at the Balls held on Thursdays during the Season. Amongst these may be mentioned:

> "That the Ball do begin at eight o'clock and finish at twelve precisely, even in the middle of a dance.
> "That after a lady has called a dance when it is finished her place in the next dance is at the bottom.
> "That two sets for Country Dances be not formed until upwards of twenty couples stand up, to be then equally divided, and no person to change from one set to another."

These were obviously modelled on the regulations laid down by Beau Nash for the Bath Assembly, and the right of entry was equally stringent.

About a dozen years later the Assembly was not quite so aristocratic. Thomas Carlyle who stayed in Margate on his way to the Netherlands tells us that the company seemed to consist of "the daughters of shopkeepers, London clerks and Margate shopmen from the obscurer streets," whom he saw dancing "a rather sparse and languid kind of quadrille danced over more than half of a large floor".

These old Assembly Rooms were burnt down in 1882.

In addition to the Balls held at such well-known Assembly Rooms as those at Almack's, the Argyll Rooms, Bath, Cheltenham, Margate and elsewhere, a number of Subscription

RANELAGH

An inside view of the Rotunda

THE CASINO DE VENISE

In Holborn near Great Queen Street. Note how the male dancers have
retained their hats

A Masquerade at the Pantheon

Balls which also became known as "Assemblies" were held in hotels and other places. Though never quite so exclusive as the dances at the Assembly Rooms proper, many of them endeavoured to maintain a certain exclusiveness while others were frankly popular events open to anyone who cared to purchase the ticket.

I have one or two contemporary announcements of these dances mostly in the Richmond (Surrey) area. In one a Mr. James Brewer announces a series of weekly Subscription Balls in November and December 1804 to be held in Brewer's New Rooms, Star & Garter, Richmond Hill, under the patronage of several ladies of distinction. In addition he advertises four special Subscription Balls on an entirely new plan and under the direction of Mr. D'Egville, Ballet-master at the Opera House. The notice adds "In order to keep the Company select, no Lady or Gentleman will be admitted without a Card of Invitation from one of the Subscribers". From two old letters accompanying this announcement Mr. Brewer seems to have written to H.R.H. the Duke of York sending particulars of these Balls obviously in an attempt to secure the Duke's patronage.

From these announcements of old Assemblies it is obvious that these were nearly entirely devoted to Country Dances. In some cases the ticket admitted one Gentleman and two Ladies which suggests that even in the Regency period a man could not take the lady of his choice without a chaperone accompanying her.

As a curiosity an announcement by Mrs. Crean of her Subscription Ball at the Star & Garter, Richmond, under the patronage of the Duchess of Buccleuch, on Monday, January 7th, 1822, at 9 p.m., may be mentioned. This has a note to the effect that this will be a moonlight night, which recalls, though for a different reason, somewhat similar notices which appeared during the Zeppelin raids of the First World War.

Another leaflet of 1822 announces a series of four Assemblies run by Mr. Martin Sanderson under the patronage of H.R.H. the Duke of Clarence at the Toy Inn, Hampton Court.

I also have notices printed in 1808 of the Albion Assembly and the Friendly Assembly, both held at the London Coffee House in Ludgate Hill, apparently patronized by well-to-do city men of that period, each containing a set of rules governing the conduct of these Assemblies. In one case it laid down that each lady on entering the room will be presented with a ticket by which the order of the dancing is to be regulated and that a short intermission will be allowed at the end of every two dances for the purpose of changing partners.

Of the public Assemblies such as those held at the New Argyll Rooms, Laurent's Casino and the Casino de Venise, which to some extent corresponded to our modern Palais de Danse, it will be more convenient to refer to these later on in this volume (see page 109).

## ⋆ 4 ⋆

## SOME DANCES PRIOR TO THE
## NINETEENTH CENTURY

AT the beginning of the nineteenth century the dances in
vogue were the Minuet, the Country Dance, the Contredanse
and the Cotillon. Of these by far the most popular was the
Country Dance but the Minuet was still the ceremonial dance
at Court and was still danced at Almack's, Bath and the leading Assemblies. It is also certain that an early form of the
Waltz was to have been seen, probably as a figure in the
Contredanse, even before the more modern form was introduced about 1812. There was also, as we shall see in the next
chapter, a considerable call for Scottish Reels which continued
even down to the coming of Queen Victoria.

As these were all nineteenth-century dances a description of
their origins and early development must be given in this
book, and in order not to break the flow of the story of the
nineteenth century by too many dips into the past I am including their history prior to 1801 in this preliminary chapter.

If the nineteenth century may be called the century of the
Waltz, the eighteenth century was that of the Minuet, and as
that dance still had a certain vogue in the early years of the
century we are considering, it is necessary to say something
about it.

It is generally agreed that the Minuet (Fr. Menuet) was developed from that particular Branle of the Suite of Branles with which all Balls began in the seventeenth century, known as the "Branle de Poitou". An early version of this Branle is described by Arbeau in his *Orchesographie* (1588) and a later version by De Lauze in his *Apologie de la Danse* (1623), English translation by Joan Wildeblood (1952).

The French name "Menuet" is said to be derived from the "little steps" (*pas menus*) used, and that diligent researcher, Curt Sachs, in his *World History of the Dance* (1938), remarks that the expression "*pas menus*" was to be found as early as the fifteenth century. On the other hand it has been suggested that the name comes from "Branle à mener", which de Lauze gives as an alternative title to Branle de Poitou.

The rhythmic possibilities of this Branle seem to have attracted the composers Louis Couperin and Jean Baptiste Lully about the middle of the seventeenth century, and the latter introduced it into several ballets he composed for Louis XIV, but at first merely described it as an "air" or "symphonie", never as a "Menuet". This term was first used in his "Le Mariage Forcé" in 1664. It may be assumed that the steps for the Minuet were arranged by Pierre Beauchamp, the King's Maître de Danse.

If the Minuet were first known by that title in 1664, how are we to account for the story told by Castil-Blaze in his "*La Danse et les Ballets*" (Paris 1832) of the brilliant dancing of the Minuet by Marguerite de Valois in the sixteenth century, which so appealed to Don Juan, the Viceroy of the Low Countries, that he rode post-haste from Brussels to Paris merely to see her dance?

Castil-Blaze not only quotes this story but adds some picturesque details. He says Don Juan was so impressed with what he saw that on the journey back to Brussels he kept repeating "Que de choses dans un menuet..."—a phrase usually attributed to Marcel, who flourished in the mid-eighteenth century.

If this story be true it is very strange that Arbeau, who dearly loved a courtly dance, made no reference to the Minuet in his book. Is it possibly due to a confusion of the terms "*pas menus*" and Menuet?

In this connection is to be noted an early reference to the Minuet in "*Le Mariage de la Musique avec la Danse*" (1664). This book was an attack by Guillaume du Manoir, the "roi des violons" and the leader of the "Maîtres de Danse et Joueurs d'Instruments" against the Académie Royale de Danse, which had just been founded by Louis XIV. He belittles the competency of the Academicians, appointed by Louis, and charges them with confusing the rhythms of the Sarabande, the Chaconne and the minuet. It is curious that though throughout the book he spells the name of any dance with a capital initial letter, in the case of the Minuet he uses a small "m". Is this a mere printer's error, or does it imply that at that time it was only a generic term for a "dance of small steps", to which the name "Minuet" had not yet been limited?

I am indebted to Miss Angela Gayden of the Barber Institute of Fine Arts, Birmingham, for pursuing at my request this idea a little further. Miss Gayden points out that the *Dictionnaire de l'Ancienne Langue Française du IXième Au XV Siècles* shows that "menuet" was then used as an adjective, but not implying any sort of dance. The *Dictionnaire Etymologique de la Langue Française* says "menuet" was an adjective until the seventeenth century, when it became the name of a dance fashionable under Louis XIV.

It would appear, therefore, that there may be some truth in

Castil-Blaze's story, if we agree that he has confused "menuet" with *"pas menus"*. I firmly believe that he, in adding circumstantial details, was drawing upon his imagination. An official of the Universiteits-Bibliotheek of Amsterdam very kindly made some researches on my behalf and wrote: "There is a scholarly book on Don Juan of Austria written in the Dutch language which does not give the story . . . Brantôme (*Vie des dames galantes*) does not mention it either (in connection with Marguerite de Valois) . . . As a general rule scant credit is to be given to this kind of anecdote—an eighteenth-century storyteller for instance may have written 'dancing a minuet' simply for 'dancing'. Anachronisms of that kind are frequent."

It is also possible that Castil-Blaze misread Cahusac's brief statement on the journey of Don Juan. In his *La Danse Ancienne et Moderne* (1754) this author in one sentence states ". . . qu'un menuet dansé avec grâce etait seul capable de faire une grande réputation". (. . . that a minuet danced gracefully was in itself enough to make a great reputation.) In the next sentence "Don Juan d'Autriche, Vice-Roi des Pays-Bas, partit exprès en poste de Bruxelles et vint à Paris incognito pour voir danser à un bal de cérémonie Marguerite de Valois qui passait pour la meilleure danseuse de l'Europe." (Don Juan of Austria, Viceroy of the Low Countries, left Brussels posthaste and rode to Paris incognito to see a ceremonial ball, at which Marguerite de Valois, considered the best dancer in Europe, was dancing." It may be that Castil-Blaze assumed from the first sentence that Marguerite de Valois danced a menuet—but Cahusac does not say so.

Whatever may have been the early history of the Minuet, it is certain that it did not come into prominence and become a definite "dance form" until shortly after the middle of the seventeenth century. A little later the choregraphy of the

Minuet was brought to perfection by Louis Pécour (1655-1729) who succeeded Beauchamp as Maître de Ballet. He altered the track of the dance from an "S" to a "Z" in the principal figure. It was Pécour in all probability who arranged the "Menuet de la Cour" for use at the Court Balls as distinct from the generally more complicated Minuets introduced into the ballets. By the close of the seventeenth century, the Menuet de la Cour had displaced the Courante as the ceremonial ballroom dance, and it reigned supreme in France until the Revolution, and in England until the early years of the nineteenth century—though possibly not in so perfect a form.

What may be called the basic Minuet was very fully described and illustrated by Rameau in his *Maître à Danser* (1725) which was translated into English by John Essex, a London dancing master (1728), and more recently (1931) by Mr. Cyril Beaumont. Kellom Tomlinson, an English teacher, gave a full description in his *Art of Dancing* (1735). Magny, in his *Principes de Chorégraphie* published in Paris in 1765, shows the steps and figurations of the "Menuet de la Reine" and the "Menuet Dauphin", which had both been arranged by that famous teacher of this dance, Marcel. He also includes an arrangement of his own of the celebrated Menuet composed by Joseph Exaudet of Rouen.

If we can place any reliance on the de Gramont *Mémoires*, the Minuet was first shown in England at the Court of Charles II in 1662 by a French exile, the Marquis de Famarens. As this was two years before Lully definitely used the term "Menuet", the Marquis must have demonstrated an early form of the dance. Anyhow, it was a considerable time before the Minuet became a recognised Court Dance in England. By the early years of the eighteenth century it had, however, displaced the Coranto and had become our cere-

monial dance. Kellom Tomlinson, in his book previously referred to, devotes many pages to the Minuet but ignores the
Coranto. It is possible that in its transit across the Channel
the Minuet lost some of its subtler touches, and that the
English teachers did not all show it in the same way.

Mr. Stephen Philpot, a teacher of Lewes in Sussex, in a
little book published in 1746 entitled *An Essay on the Advantage of a Polite Education,* has the following remarks to make
on the Minuet, which show the difficulties teachers had even
in those days to know the correct version of a dance:

> Mr. Weaver, in his translation of Monsieur Feuillet, has added
> by way of Supplement all the Minuet steps that may have been
> taught by the best Masters in our own and other Countries, since
> this dance was invented. But which of those steps should be
> taught, and in what part of the Dance introduced, wants to be
> more generally agreed upon and settled, for that is a point in
> which several very good Masters differ to mention the various
> ways of beginning the Minuet, performing the steps and the
> many Whims that are used as Graces in it and take up too much
> room and not answer any purpose.

Paris in the days of Louis XVI was the hub of the dancing
world and polite society in all European countries looked to
Versailles and the French Court for their fashionable dances.
In England among the higher classes the French Court dances
were the vogue. But here there were signs that other dances
were being done.

From the advertisements of the day we read that at the
one-time fashionable Carlisle House in Soho Square "a new
gallery for the dancing of Cotillons and Allemandes, and a
suite of new rooms adjoining" were opened in January 1769.
Two years later an advertisement in a London newspaper of
March 19th, 1771, referring to the Annual Ball to be given by

a well-known teacher of the day, Mr. Yates, at Carlisle House, announced that:

> After the Minuet, Cotillions and Allemands are danced by his scholars, there will be a Ball for the Company. There will be refreshments of Tea, Coffee, Lemonade, Orgeat, Biscuits etc. and music in a different room for those who chose to make sets for Cotillions etc., before the scholars have finished.

To appreciate how the change from the cold and stately Minuet to the warm and circling Waltz came to pass, we must look back a few years into the eighteenth century, to the outbreak of the French Revolution in 1789.

Louis XVI and Marie Antoinette were King and Queen of France, and at the magnificent balls they gave in the Palace of Versailles or elsewhere the Minuet and other courtly dances were supreme.

The Minuet at the time of the French Revolution was over one hundred years old as a Court Dance, and signs were not wanting that it had outlived its day. Originally a mid-seventeenth-century attempt to symbolise the chivalry of the Middle Ages and to revive the ideology of the Troubadours and Minnesingers, it had become towards the close of the eighteenth century a mirror of the artificial courtesies and the rich costumes seen at the Court of the Bourbons, out of touch with the romanticism which was already beginning to permeate the bourgeoisie of Europe, who for their dances were turning to folk and peasant song for inspiration. The livelier, more sociable and warm-blooded dances of the people crept into the houses of the bourgeoisie and, as the Contredanse, invaded the Court. This was a stepping-stone towards the inclusion of the still more intimate Waltz, which was then almost unknown.

In France the Revolution struck a mortal blow at the Minuet and other Court Dances, and their stately measures gave way for a time to the strains of "Ca Ira" and the "Carmagnole".

### The Waltz

The Waltz, in what may be called its "allemande" form, that is with entwining arm-movements but without the close hold, was undoubtedly known in England a number of years before 1812, and as such was probably used as a figure of a Cotillon or Contredanse. The word "waltz" simply means to turn, and the modern dance is derived from a turning dance of the peasants. This is generally agreed, but there has been considerable argument as to which particular form of this old turning dance was the immediate ancestor of the modern waltz. Many French writers, led by Castil-Blaze a hundred years ago, claim that it is a direct descendant possibly of the Galliard but more probably of the Volta. This latter dance came from a turning dance of Provence, and it was described by Thoinot Arbeau in his *Orchesographie* as long ago as 1588. The old Canon obviously does not approve of the dance, owing to the rather indelicate movements used and the whirling action required, and fears that it "assails both the honour and the health of the lady". Nevertheless, the Volta found favour at the French Court and in England. It is mentioned by Shakespeare.

"They bid us to the English dancing schools and teach lavoltas high and swift corantos."

and both Queen Elizabeth I and Mary Queen of Scots were enthusiastic performers. There is a well-known painting at Penshurst Place in Kent of Queen Elizabeth doing the Volta with the Earl of Leicester. And there is another picture showing a couple dancing La Volta in the Museum at Rennes attributed to Herman Van Der Mast (c.1570). About 1650 the Volta was banned at the French Court.

In spite of the French claim it is now more generally accepted that the immediate ancestor of our modern Waltz was to be found among the "turning" dances which were so prevalent in Germany. We hear of many of these under different names, particularly the Dreher, which was danced in Upper Bavaria and the Landler which came from the Landl or "little country" lying to the west of Austria, abutting on Switzerland and Alsace.

It is interesting to note that the English writer, Thomas Wilson in 1816 wrote:

> Waltzing is a species of dancing that owes its origin to the Germans, having been introduced in Swabia, one of the nine circles of Germany.

Carlo Blasis, the Italian, a few years later thought that it came from Switzerland.

Curt Sachs in his *World History of the Dance* (1938) quotes a poem by Nicolaus Lenau, entitled "Der Steyrertanz" which gives a graphic description of the Landler. From this it appears that each couple makes a number of circling movements under raised arms which are entwined in different ways, and that it is only towards the close of the dance that the partners come together in close embrace.

This at once suggests the Allemande or Deutscher, and it might be noted that Swabia was once known as Alemannia. Moreover the Reference Plate at the beginning of Wilson's *Description of the Correct method of Waltzing* shows couples dancing with arm positions which bear a strong resemblance to the positions shown in Dubois' *Principes d'Allemande*. In none is a couple shown in close embrace.

Edwin Evans in his *Music and the Dance* had some very instructive remarks to make on the Waltz:

> When waltzes were first danced in Vienna only common people indulged in them, their "betters" pointedly abstaining . . . In Prague, more democratic than Vienna, the waltz became quickly fashionable until in 1785 it was banned by an Imperial Edict.
>
> Vienna . . . is the true birthplace of the waltz as an urban dance. It was therefore quite legitimately called at first Deutscher Tanz, German Dance, or simply Deutscher. It was Vienna which first developed the music of the waltz and remained for a century the source of its best examples. Mozart was appointed Kammersmusikus to the Emperor in 1787, and began composing the following year for the Redouten. He wrote no dances specifically described as waltzes but . . . contributed fifty Deutscher and six Landler, which are virtually the same dance in its original form. Beethoven composed in November 1795 twelve Deutscher for the Redoutensaal.

The waltz probably made its first appearance on the stage in 1787 in Vincent Martin's opera "Una Causa Rara". In 1800 it was definitely danced in a ballet by Gardel in "La Dansomanie".

A popular waltz tune towards the close of the eighteenth century was "Ach! Du lieber Augustin", which was revived in England about thirty years ago as the air for the "Frothblowers" Chorus—"The More we are Together". These early waltz tunes were frequently in 3/8 or 6/8 time, played rather slowly. In turning, the peasant dancers in all probability lifted their feet, and it was not until the Waltz reached the polished floors of Vienna—where the dancers wore light footwear instead of the heavy shoes of the country folk—that it became a gliding dance.

A very clear and interesting description of how the waltz was danced in Germany in the second half of the eighteenth century will be found in the *Story of the Waltz* by Dr. Eduard Reeser, one of the Symphonia Books which deal with the history of music. This has been translated from the Dutch by W. A. G. Doyle-Davidson and is published in England by Sidgwick & Jackson of London. The author points out that by the end of the eighteenth century the waltz "had already moved away from the movements which had become traditional in the Landler, such as the revolving of the lady beneath the raised hands of her stamping partner, etc.". The waltz, it appears, was danced more quickly than the Landler, though its steps were the same. At first it was confined to the common people and seems to have been danced with a considerable amount of indelicacy, and as a result it was officially banned in several countries.

### Country Dance, Contredanse, Cotillon

Throughout the eighteenth century the Country Dance increased in popularity in the English Ballroom, and at the famous Bath Assemblies presided over by Beau Nash, and at similar Assemblies elsewhere, it always followed the Minuets on Ball Nights.

These Country Dances were essentially of English origin. They came from the people and it is impossible to say with any accuracy when they began. They were first described in print by John Playford in his book *The English Dancing Master* in 1651, in which are to be found over one hundred examples. This was only a few years before Oliver Cromwell was declared Lord Protector, and the ready sale rather belies the modern impression that during the Commonwealth dancing was looked at askance. The book was reprinted as *The*

*Dancing Master* about seventeen times between 1651 and about 1728, each new edition containing further dances, and there were also one or two composite editions.

In its early days the Country Dance had several forms. There was for instance the Round, such as "Sellenger's Round", one of the very oldest of our dances. There was the Square-Eight form, such as King Charles II's favourite dance, "Cuckolds all A-Wry", and there was the Longways dance such as "Greensleeves". Gradually this latter form displaced the others in popularity and when we come to its introduction into France we shall see that Feuillet described only the Longways.

In the Longways Country Dance there were two parallel lines—the men in one and the ladies in the other—and by the end of each figure the leading couple passed down the line one place, the end of the dance coming when they had reached the bottom and returned to the top again, each other couple having taken the lead in turn. They were described as "longways for as many as will", and could be danced by any number of couples in excess of two.

There were several variations of the Longways Dance. When the number of couples was small, say up to eight, the "Whole Set" could be treated as one entity; when there were a considerable number of couples the dancers were divided into "Minor Sets", either "Duple Minor" (two couples) or "Triple Minor" (three couples). In these cases the same principle of passing down the set was maintained, and sometimes all couples were dancing at once, and on other occasions a number had to "stand easy".

The dances were named after the tunes to which they were danced, and at the beginning of each dance the leading lady had the privilege of calling the tune.

The fullest description of the Country Dance as done in the nineteenth century will be found in the works of Thomas Wilson, a London dance teacher. It must be admitted that he is somewhat difficult to follow, but one gathers that a good dancer must have a knowledge of the configurations used in a considerable number of dances, and the steps to be used for each movement. Compare this with the great number of Old Time and Sequence Dances whose configuration is known to the Old Time dancer of today. The most frequently used steps appear to have been the chassé, the jeté and the assemblé. Great care had to be taken by the lady calling the dance that the music fitted the selected figures. It will, therefore, be realised how essential it was that the Master of Ceremonies, on whose advice she would have to rely, should be an accomplished Country Dancer.

The English Country Dance was introduced into France towards the close of the seventeenth century and found some favour even at the Court of Louis XIV, where it was known as the Contredanse Anglaise.

This introduction of a lively dance as a foil to the rigid etiquette of the Court Dances is not surprising. The history of dancing shows that in every age it has been the habit of the younger generation to chafe against the dances of their fathers and for the latter to bemoan the alleged decadence of the Art. We have, ourselves, seen this happen in the twentieth century, just as it happened over two hundred years ago, when in 1724, Bonnet in his *Histoire de la Danse* wrote:

Since the marriage of M. le Duc de Bourgogne it is noticeable that the noble and serious dances such as the Canaries, the Passepied, the Duchesse and many others which showed to such advantage the grace and elegance of the "danse grave" are from year to year being dropped. The Branle, the Courante and the

Minuet have with difficulty held their place, the young people of the Court having substituted Contredanses in which one can see no more the dignity and nobility of former times as it was practised in the days of the old Court. Such are La Jalousie, the Cotillion, Greensleeves, Les Rats, the Cabaretière, the Testard, the Rémouleur etc., so that as time goes on we shall only have these "danses baladines" during our ceremonial assemblies. This encourages the destruction of serious dancing and confirms the reproach of the changing humour of the French who in this, as in many other things, sacrifice good things for the sake of novelty.

In 1706 Raoul Auger Feuillet, a Paris dancing master, published a number of these dances "longways for as many as will", giving a description of the movements and a reproduction of the tunes to which they were danced. Many of the described dances can be found in the tenth edition of *The Dancing Master* (1698), others were probably arranged by the author himself on similar lines. In the preface to this book he makes the very definite statement that these dances were of English origin.

In France after the first quarter of the eighteenth century the Contredanse Anglaise seems to have been replaced by the Contredanse Française, known simply as the "contredanse", and the Cotillon. These two dances are historically of considerable importance, as from them came the Quadrille and all the modern square dances. It is exceedingly difficult to describe with any confidence their early history, and the difficulty is increased because many of the old writers used the terms indiscriminately. For instance Compan in his *Dictionnaire* (1787) dismisses "Les Cotillons" (he uses the plural) merely as the name of a Contredanse.

The Cotillon was probably, in the beginning, a simple French peasant dance for a number of couples dancing possibly in a circle which later became a square. We first hear

THE DANCING-PLATFORM AT CREMORNE IN 1847

Almack's
The Opening of the Season

of it at the time of Louis XIV. It was based on peasant airs and may have been equivalent to the English "Round". The name literally means "under-petticoat" and comes from the words of one of the earliest tunes to which it was danced:

"Ma Commère, quand je danse
Mon Cotillon va-t-il bien?"

The Contredanse was also a square dance for two or four couples and was possibly derived from the "Duple Minor" set of the English Country Dance by the French dancing masters of the period. Indeed it may be suggested that the Contredanse savoured more of the dancing master and less of the simple movements of the country folk than did the cotillon. These Contredanses have been described by, amongst others, Landrin in 1750 and Vincent in 1780. About this latter date Dubois of the Opera published his *Principes d'Allemandes* and at the end of this work are several dances described as Contredanses Allemandes.

Both Contredanses and Cotillons were danced in England at the close of the eighteenth century and during the early years of the nineteenth. About that time there was published by Messrs. Randall and Abell, successors to the late Mr. Walsh in Catherine Street, Strand, a little book of "Sixteen Cotillons or French Dances as performed at Court and all Polite Assemblies". From the description each Cotillon is for four couples and it is interesting to note that in one, "Le Point du Jour", the Minuet step is indicated in a portion of the dance. In another handclapping is introduced.

That Cotillon which found favour in France and England in the second half of the nineteenth century, consisting of many figures in which favours were distributed, forfeits paid and

4

many properties used, was really a dancing game and will be referred to later (page 99).

The modern Valse Cotillon which still finds favour at Old Time Assemblies, if not a true descendant of the old dance, certainly has been suggested by it.

# ★ 5 ★

## THE EARLY YEARS (1801-1815)

THE nineteenth century opened in those disturbing days which followed the French Revolution when the rise of Napoleon to power threatened the peace of Europe. Its earliest years witnessed a serious threat of invasion from his Grand Army gathered on the cliffs of Boulogne, a threat dissipated by the victories of the English fleet under Lord Nelson. The second decade saw the French driven from Spain by Wellington in the Peninsular campaign, Napoleon's disastrous retreat from Moscow and surrender after Leipzig, and it was not until the middle of this decade in 1815, after Bonaparte had escaped from Elba, that the victory of Waterloo brought peace to Europe.

Undoubtedly these tremendous happenings on the Continent in which our professional army was engaged did not affect the social life of this country in the same way as did the total first and second World Wars. We could scarcely picture King George VI and Queen Elizabeth giving a grand ball at Buckingham Palace to celebrate the victory of El Alamein. In 1813, however, to commemorate the successful Battle of Vittoria in the Peninsular War, the Prince Regent gave a very big Ball. This was held in Carlton House, the magnificent London home of the Regent, which stood on the site of the present Carlton House Terrace overlooking the Mall.

The ball was also made the occasion of the "coming out" of the Princess Charlotte, the only daughter of the Regent and then about sixteen years of age. Captain Gronow of the Grenadier Guards, who saw active service in the Peninsular and Waterloo campaigns, in his book *Reminiscences and Recollections*, has the following remark to make about this ball, which throws an interesting light on the dances then in favour at any rate in Court circles:

> The Princess Charlotte honoured with her presence two dances. In the first she accepted the hand of the late Duke of Devonshire and in the second, that of the Earl of Aboyne, who had danced with Marie Antoinette and who, as Lord Huntley, lived long enough to dance with Queen Victoria. The Princess entered so much into the spirit of the Fête as to ask for the then fashionable Scotch Dances.

This enthusiasm for Scottish dances was due probably to the fact that in 1781 the Act of Proscription had been repealed. This Act, made in 1746 after Culloden, amongst other things forbade the wearing of the kilt. Its repeal, together with the influence of the poems and novels of Sir Walter Scott and the enthusiasm for the Scottish soldiers who did so well in the Napoleonic Campaigns, led to this revival of interest in Scottish dancing both in Scotland and England. The fact that Almack's, the most fashionable Assembly Rooms in London, were owned by a Scotsman and that a famous Scottish band, Neil Gow's, played there would undoubtedly encourage this revival.

During the first decade of the century at Almack's the Minuet, the Country Dance, Cotillon and Contredanse found favour, and Scotch Reels and the Écossaise were much in evidence.

The Écossaise was a popular dance during this period. It seems to have been a lively and spirited measure in 2/4 time, partaking partly of the nature of a Reel and partly of a Country Dance, in which each gentleman at some movement took two partners at the same time. In spite of its name, this Écossaise was definitely of French origin, though Scottish music was used. Indeed that well known modern authority on Scottish dances, Mr. D. G. MacLennan, states it was not generally known in Scotland. On the other hand, in Grove's *Dictionary of Music* it is claimed that it was, in earlier days, danced in Scotland, accompanied by the bagpipes. It is of course, possible that this original Écossaise was imported into France by Jacobite refugees after 1745. Although little is known about this dance, it undoubtedly had a considerable influence on our dances, and Schubert and Beethoven both composed a number of Écossaises for the piano.

In Tolstoi's *War and Peace* there is a description of a great ball in Russia held at the beginning of the nineteenth century at which the Écossaise was in considerable demand. A fairly detailed description of the dance will be found at page 438 of Curt Sachs *World History of the Dance*.

I have already pointed out how the minuet and other Court dances were not danced any more in France after the revolution. It is true that in 1814, with the restoration of the Bourbons, there was an attempt made by the old nobility to revive these dances. The enthusiasm for the revival was, however, confined to the elders; the young folk had never known these dances, and preferred the more modern introductions.

Captain Gronow, in his *Reminiscences and Recollections* (1810-1860), refers to a then famous restaurant on the Boulevards in Paris known as Tortoni's to which came the old aristocracy. On one occasion the Princess de Beauvau invited those who were present to meet at her Hotel at midnight to dance.

> On our arrival we were agreeably surprised to find Mousard, Colinet and other musicians assembled, and ready to strike up a Quadrille or a Waltz. In those days the Minuet, Gavotte and Monaco were the favourite dances, and if a gentleman could master sufficient grace and agility for any of the fashionable dances, he was sure of receiving invitations from the best houses in the Faubourg Saint Germain.

The Monaco mentioned in this quotation seems to have attained some popularity in France after the Revolution. It was a lively dance in 2/4 time, somewhat of the nature of a Cotillon, to which the following words were sung:

> A la Monaco
> L'on chasse
> Et l'on déchasse
> A la Monaco
> L'on danse comme il faut

In all my old books this is the only reference I can find to this dance, but there has, within the last few years, been published in France by Dumas of Saint-Étienne (Loire) a book entitled *Dansez la France* which contains words, music and a description of the dance.

In England during the first decade of the nineteenth century, though the country dance was still the most popular item of all programmes, the minuet had a certain vogue. It was still the ceremonial dance at the Court Balls, and for a time it was danced at Almack's, at Bath and at many of the more exclusive Assemblies.

Mr. G. Yates, probably a relation of the Mr. Yates whose advertisement has been quoted, in 1829 published a book entitled *The Ball: or a Glance at Almack's,* in which he regrets the abolition of the St. James's Palace Birthnight Balls and the consequent decay in the style of dancing. By the time the book was written George IV was on the throne, but the author gives a very interesting description of the Minuet as danced at these famous Court Balls in the previous reign. These Balls came to an end when the declining health of George III made it impossible for him to attend. It will be remembered that he became permanently insane about 1811, though he did not die until 1820.

On Their Majesties entrance, the Court Band stationed in the Music Gallery at the opposite end of the room, commenced playing the March from *Judas Maccabeus* (See the Conquering Hero Comes) which by the King's command was always performed on this occasion. After Their Majesties had walked around the inside of the space set apart, and had spoken a few words with those of the Nobility that were near enough, they retired to their chairs (for there was no throne), and this was the signal for the Band to cease. Then the Lord Chamberlain advanced to the Prince of Wales and his Royal sister, making his obeisance before them, on which they arose and performed the same ceremony before Their Majesties, retiring backwards until they arrived at the opposite end of the open space, when the Band immediately commenced playing a Minuet.

The Court Dancing Master (M. Desnoyer), spread the Lady's train, which was exceedingly long and heavy with gold or silver, and which, during the respectful preliminary, had been supported by the hoop. Having concluded a Minuet the obeisance was repeated to Their Majesties; and in the same manner proceeded the other members of the Royal Family and Nobility according to precedence, going through the same ceremonies. A Country Dance or two followed when the Minuets were over; for Cotillons or Quadrilles were not then in fashion at Court.

When the Birthnight Balls were no longer held, the Minuet

gradually passed away, never to make any serious return to our Ballrooms.

Canon Sheppard in his *Memorials of St. James's Palace* (1894) quotes a long poem by one C. M. Fanshawe, entitled "Elegy on the Abrogation of the Birth-Night Ball and consequent final Subversion of the Minuet", which included the following lines:

> "No more the well-taught feet shall tread
> The figures of the Mazy Zed;
> The beau of other times shall mourn,
> As gone and never to return,
> The graceful bow, the curtesey low,
> The floating forms that undulating glide
> (Like anchored vessels on the swelling tide)
> That rise and sink, alternate as they go,
> Now bent the knee, now lifted on the toe,
> The sidelong step that works it even way,
> The slow 'pas grave' and slower 'balancé'.
>
> Be mine to trace the minuet's fate
> And weep its fallen glory.
>
> In vain—these eyes, with tears of horror wet
> Read its death warrant in the 'Court Gazette'.
> 'No ball to-night!' Lord Chamberlain proclaims;
> 'No ball to-night shall grace thy roof, St. James!'
> 'No ball?' the 'Globe', the 'Sun', the 'Star' repeat
> The morning papers and the evening sheet;
> Through all the land the tragic news has spread
> And all the land has mourned the minuet dead."

The Birthnight Balls were very occasionally revived, but without the Minuet. In 1831 King William and Queen Adelaide gave one in honour of the twelfth birthday of Princess Victoria, and in 1837, shortly before she ascended the throne, a similar Ball in honour of her birthday was given at which the Princess danced the Quadrille with Lord Fitzalan, and other dances with Prince Esterhazy and Prince William of Saxe-Weimar.

As already pointed out, during the eighteenth century the most popular dance in England was the Country Dance which was to be found prominently featured by all grades of society.

During the early years of the nineteenth century it was still a great favourite. It was danced at the Court Balls, it was to be seen at Almack's, and figures prominently at all the Public Assemblies where, though according to Thomas Wilson very badly danced, it was associated with rigid etiquette.

Before the middle of the century the increasing popularity of the Quadrille and the more intimate Waltz and the invasion of our ballrooms by the Polka swept the Country Dance off the floor.

The only one that lingered and remained popular, particularly as a "finishing dance" was "Sir Roger de Coverley" and long before the end of the century even this had been relegated to Christmas and children's parties. In America, however, this particular dance survived for a long time as the Virginia Reel, and here to avoid long periods of inaction the full set was divided into "Duple Minor" sets, so that all couples were dancing all the time.

The Contredanse, and to some extent the Cotillon are, as already mentioned, of great historical interest, because it was from these dances that the set known as the Quadrille was formed. Towards the close of the eighteenth century and the beginning of the nineteenth in France, the terms Contredanse and Quadrille were almost interchangeable. As early as 1765 Magny in his *Principes de Chorégraphie* includes a set of exercises which embody all the movements used in Contredanses. This he calls a Quadrille, and Gourdoux-Daux in his *De l'Art de la Danse* (1823) to be subsequently quoted, heads his article on the Quadrille, "Description méthodique des figures de Contredanse." Gradually, however, when a single figure was done it was called by the old name, but when several Contredanses were danced in succession by the same sets, the term Quadrille was used. There was published in Paris a book of music entitled *Étrennes à Terpsichore, Contredanses, Valses et Écossaises pour le Piano* by one Henri Lemoine. Each Contredanse is given a name, such as "L'Aldino", "La Rosalinda". There is no mention of the word Quadrille, but under each dance, in lieu of a description of the movements, appears the name of one of the recognised figures of the Quadrille. Under "L'Aldino" for instance appears "Figure du Pantalon" and under "La Rosalinda" is printed "Figure de l'Été". On the other hand Wilson, in his *Quadrille Panorama*, 1822, whilst agreeing that the Quadrille was entirely of French origin, says it is derived from the Cotillon.

Four or five of the most popular Contredanses of the day form the basis of the Quadrille, as danced in Paris in the early years of the nineteenth century. It would appear that Lady Jersey must have visited Paris and being impressed by these Quadrilles decided to introduce them to London society. As she was perhaps the most formidable of the Lady Patrons who ruled Almack's almost with a rod of iron she had little difficulty in making the necessary arrangements and the Quadrilles were danced by eight specially picked couples at Almack's in 1815.

Captain Gronow, whose regiment was quartered in Portman Street at the time, wrote:

> I recollect the persons who formed the very first Quadrille that was ever danced at Almack's. They were Lady Jersey, Lady

Harriet Butler, Lady Susan Ryde and Miss Montgomery; the men being the Count St. Aldegonde, Mr. Montgomery, Mr. Montague and Charles Standish.

At first the Quadrille was made up of four of the most popular Contredanses of the day. There were Pantalon, L'Été, La Poule and La Trenis. Later on a fifth or final figure was added, and this it seems was definitely derived from the Cotillon. Probably the Quadrille introduced by Lady Jersey consisted of the above mentioned four figures without the finale. La Pastourelle, the figure which subsequently displaced La Trenis, was first danced in 1812 and until 1835 was used as an alternative figure, but after that year La Trenis was practically ignored.

Apart from its having been the name of a very old game of cards, the word "quadrille" had been associated in France with dancing and pageantry for many years.

Compan in his *Dictionnaire de la Danse* (1787) says the Quadrille was originally a small company of cavalry, superbly mounted and equipped, which appeared in the old jousts, tourneys and carousels. The name is derived from the Italian and is a diminutive of the word "squadra", a company of soldiers formed in a square. Later on the word was used to denote a group of dancers in a pageant and, when on the stage, usually all dressed alike, and constituting one of the "entrées" in a ballet.

It will be readily understood that as there were a very great number of Contredanses and Cotillons it would have been possible to form many different sets of Quadrilles. Paine of Almack's published a set of cards for the use of Masters of Ceremony, small enough to be held in the palm of the hand, describing sixteen different sets. In actual practice, however, by far the most important was that known as the "First Set".

This was the set introduced by Lady Jersey, on which our modern Quadrille is based. It was derived from four of the most popular Contredanses of the period. These were : (1) La Chaîne Anglaise or Le Pantalon. This is said to have been invented in 1786 by Vincent, later on the accompanist of the great Taglioni. Desrat in his *Dictionnaire de la Danse*, published in 1895, claims that the alternative title "Le Pantalon" came into use in 1830 when Louis-Philippe came to the throne after the Revolution of that year, and Mr. Edward Scott, usually so careful, falls into the error of accepting this. But Desrat must always be checked and there are books published ten years earlier (1820) which call the first figure "Le Pantalon".

Desrat's erroneous statement was probably due to the fact that Vincent, the inventor, was given permission to wear trousers (pantalons) when appearing at Court Balls. He, therefore, became known as Vincent Pantalon, and the figure was named after his second nickname.

As a matter of fact, just as the Cotillon had been named after one of the airs to which it was originally danced, so was this figure which was danced to a tune bearing the refrain.

> Le Pantalon
> De Toinon
> N'a pas de fond. . . . etc.

(2) The second figure received its name from a contredanse also invented by Vincent in use in the year 1800, made up of a combination of somewhat difficult steps commonly known at the time as Pas d'été afterwards simplified though the name was retained.

(3) Vincent called the Contredanse selected for the third figure, La Poule, as at one moment the music resembled the clucking of hens.

(4) La Trenis is named after the eccentric originator of that figure. The figure which subsequently displaced it, La Pastourelle, commemorates "Gentille Pastourelle", a ballad of the day by the cornet player Collinet which had met with immense success.

The fifth or final figure has been danced in many ways. About 1832, for instance, one variation popular in Paris made free use of the Galop. This was called "La Saint-Simonienne", as it included a change of partners, thus suggesting the strange marriage views of the French philosopher of that period, Saint-Simon. Other variations in favour were known as "La Boulangère", "Chassé-croisé", and "La Corbeille". The Finale in general use today appears to be derived from "La Boulangère".

There have been other sets of Quadrilles, as already stated, but few of these have achieved more than a temporary popularity.

The dance, unlike the Waltz, was welcomed by London Society with open arms, and by the time Queen Victoria came to the throne it was established as the ceremonial Court Dance.

In a periodical called the *Northern Looking Glass* there appeared on Monday, November the 28th, 1825, some drawings by William Heath of the various figures of a set of Quadrilles. This particular set was made up of (1) Le Pantalon, (2) L'Été, (3) La Poule, (4) La Trenis and a final figure. The description of the figures is attributed to a Monsieur Boulogne, but whether this is a fictitious name or not it is impossible to say. The illustrations which are reproduced in this periodical form a delightful caricature of the costume of the period.

When first introduced in England in 1815, extremely complicated and difficult steps were used by some of the dancers, as the following story of an episode at Almack's, told by Captain Gronow shows:

> The late Lord Graves, who was extremely fat, but who danced well for his size, engaged the beautiful Lady Harriet Butler one evening as his partner in a quadrille. Her Ladyship had just arrived from Paris where she had been brought up under the auspices of Josephine, and having received lessons in dancing from the celebrated Vestris, she electrified the English with the graceful ease with which she made her entrechats, so much so that a circle was generally formed to admire her dancing. Lord Graves, desirous of doing his utmost to please his fair partner, ventured on imitating the lady's entrechat, but, in making the attempt, he unluckily fell heavily to the floor. Nothing daunted, he got on his feet again, and finished the Quadrille as well as he could, when his friends hastened to sympathise with him. But Sir John Clarke in a sarcastic manner said, "What could have induced you at your age and in your state to make so great a fool of yourself as to attempt an entrechat?"

Gronow goes on to tell how it was only by the good offices of Lord Sefton, who had witnessed the incident, that a duel was avoided and that all ended happily.

This inclusion of difficult steps is substantiated by Thomas Wilson, in his "Quadrille and Cotillon Panorama", published in 1822, in which he stated that the steps used in Quadrilles included sissones, coupés, balotés, balancés, rigadoons, emboîts, chassés, jetés, assemblés, glissades, pas de basque, "although professed dancers for the sake of variety often introduce other steps than the above-named".

I am inclined to take Mr. Wilson's statement with a grain of salt and to believe that these difficult steps were only used by a few accomplished dancers who wished to "show off". Certain contemporary literature suggests that the quadrilles could be danced by anyone who had a knowledge of two or three of the simplest steps used in dancing.

I have already referred to the fact that waltz music was well-known in England for a number of years prior to the beginning of the nineteenth century, and that in its "allemande" form, that is to say with intertwining arms, but no "close hold", it was probably used as a figure in a contredanse or cotillon. In its more intimate form with a close hold, as we known it to-day, it was first seen at Almack's about 1812, introduced in all probability by travelled aristocrats who had seen it on the Continent where, as was to be the case in England, it met with very strenuous opposition.

It would seem that the dancing profession of this country, particularly Mr. Thomas Wilson, wished the waltz to retain its allemande form and that they did not approve of the custom, which probably arose in Germany, of cutting out all these beautiful arm movements and supplanting them all with a close hold as more or less seen today. It must be remembered that this was probably the first time the close hold had ever been seen in an English ballroom and, just as the supposed indelicacies of the modern tango shocked England exactly 100 years later, so did the equally supposed indelicacies of the waltz shock Regency England.

The following quotations will give a very clear idea of the type of waltz which found favour in the west end of London from about the year 1812, in spite of the tremendous outcry against the possible indelicacies of the new dances.

Lord Byron, a bitter opponent of this dance, in a letter which precedes his poem "The Waltz", written under the pseudonym "Horace Hornem", describes how he

"Went to a ball at the Countess's expecting to see a Country Dance, or at most Cotillons, Reels and all the old faces to the

newest tunes, but judge of my surprise on entering to see poor
dear Mrs. Hornem with her arms half round the loins of a huge
hussar-looking gentleman I never set eyes on before; and his, to
say truth, rather more than half round her waist, turning round
and round to a d . . . d see-saw up-and-down sort of tune till it
made me quite giddy with wondering they were not so. By and
by they stopped and I thought they would sit or fall down—but
no; with Mrs. H's hand on his shoulder, quam familiarita (as
Terence said when I was at school) they walked about a minute,
and then at it again, like two cockchafers spitted on the same
bodkin."

In Captain Gronow's *Reminiscences and Recollections* we
read that:

In 1814 the dances at Almack's were Scotch reels and the old
English Country Dance; and the orchestra, being from
Edinburgh, was conducted by the then celebrated Neil Gow*.
It was not until 1815 that Lady Jersey introduced from Paris the
favourite Quadrille, which has so long remained popular . . . The
"Mazy Waltz" was also brought to us about this time, but there
were comparatively few who at first ventured to whirl round
the salons of Almack's; in course of time Lord Palmerston might,
however, have been seen describing an infinite number of circles
with Madame de Lieven. Baron de Neumann was frequently
seen perpetually turning with the Princess Esterhazy; and in
course of time the waltzing mania, having turned the heads of
Society generally, descended to their feet and the Waltz was
practised in the morning in certain noble mansions in London
with unparalleled assiduity.

It is a little strange that in his book *A Description of the
correct method of Waltzing*, published 1816, Mr. Wilson
makes no reference at all to this latter form, but in all prob-

---

* Captain Gronow may have heard Neil Gow's orchestra, but he cannot
have seen the celebrated Neil himself, as that famous player of Scotch
Reels, who was born at Inver near Dunkeld in 1727, died there in 1807.
Doubtless his orchestra was carried on by one of his four sons.

At Almack's in 1815

Beau Brummel talking to the Duchess of Rutland, Comte de St. Antonio dancing with Princess Esterhazy, Sir George Warrender and Count St. Aldigonde

EARLY WALTZ STEPS

From the explanatory plate in Thomas Wilson's *Treatise on Waltzing* (1816)

ability he did not at that time number many members of the upper classes among his pupils—a probability that is borne out by the list of subscribers published in the volume in question, as these are mostly drawn from the dancers at the King's Theatre, Theatre Royal Drury Lane, Theatre Royal Covent Garden, Astley's Royal Amphitheatre, the Aquatic Theatre at Sadler's Wells and the Royalty and Strand Theatres. Under the stringent class-distinctions then in vogue, none of these people would be admitted to any of the smart assemblies of the day, such as Almack's or Bath. Wilson was also a staunch supporter of the Country Dance and what, to-day, we should call Old Time and established measures, and would look askance at this modern innovation.

Writing in 1829 Mr. G. Yates, the dancing master, in his book from which I have already quoted, makes a reference to the Waltz which is of some interest owing to the mention of the Allemande.

> The Waltz, when well danced to a gentle measure, is one of the most graceful of dances—as interesting, or nearly so, as the Allemande dance; but the fashionable scamper that has now usurped the name, is neither Waltz, Sauteuse, Polonaise nor anything that can legitimately be styled a dance. It is nothing in short but an outright romp, as destitute of figure or variety as the motion of a horse in a mill.

In spite of all the opposition and in spite of the bad way in which it was first danced, the more intimate form of the Waltz seems to have made steady progress in this country, first of all capturing Society and gradually permeating all classes of Assembly.

# ★ 6 ★

## AFTER WATERLOO (1815-1860)

WE have seen that in the early years of the century the minuet was rapidly falling into abeyance and that the fashionable dances were the English Country Dance, the French Quadrille, the French Contredanse or Cotillon, and the German Waltz. We have also gathered from Captain Gronow's remarks that at any rate in the second decade of the century, and probably earlier, at the very exclusive Assemblies at Almack's, Scottish Reels were very popular and that a Scottish orchestra from Edinburgh played at these Balls. Later on we shall find that these Scottish dances were in great favour in the early days of Queen Victoria.

This may be an opportune moment to include a few words on costume which in the closing years of the eighteenth and the early years of the nineteenth century underwent great changes both in the case of women and men. The billowing polonaise with its hooped panniers which we associate with the closing years of the minuet began to fall into disuse after 1780. For a year or so the bustle still found favour but just before the close of the eighteenth century the fashionable world turned to Ancient Greece for its inspiration, and we had long clinging skirts and an exceedingly high waistline known as the Empire style. By the time of the first quadrille in England skirts were becoming a little fuller and of ankle length thus making some of the intricate steps sometimes used in that set easier to execute. By 1790 the very artificial puffing up and powdering of the hair had ceased and the natural hair was arranged at the top of the head with soft curls. In the 1780's men's wigs which had been built up by the Macaronis of ten years earlier to extravagant heights began to be discarded, and after a brief period of powdered hair the natural hair came into its own. The greatest change in evening wear was perhaps the substitution of trousers for knee breeches, and of this change Captain Gronow in his Reminiscences has an amusing story to tell. In 1816, he was stationed in Paris and, to use his own words :

> As I went out a great deal into the world and was every night at some ball or party, I found that knee-breeches were only worn by a few old fogies; trousers and shoes being the usual costume of all the young men of the day. I returned to London with Hervey Aston, towards the end of the year, and we put up at Fenton's in St. James's Street.
>
> I mention the following somewhat trivial circumstances to give some notion of the absurd severity in matters of dress and etiquette of Brummel's worthy pupil, the Prince Regent. A few days after my arrival, I received an invitation to a party at Manchester House, from Lady Hertford, "to have the honour of meeting the Prince."
>
> I went there dressed à la Française and quite correctly, as I imagined, with white neckcloth and waistcoat, and black trousers, shoes, and silk stockings. The Prince had dined there, and I found him in the octagon-room, surrounded by all the great ladies of the Court. After making my bow, and retiring to the further part of the room, I sat down by the beautiful Lady Heathcote, and had been engaged in conversation with her for some time, when Horace Seymour tapped me on the shoulder and said "The 'great man', meaning the Prince, "is very much

the salon. From the beginning one saw that there was, in this ence without knee-breeches. He considers it as a want of proper respect for him."

This very disagreeable hint drove me away from Manchester House in a moment, in no very pleasant mood, as may be imagined; and I much fear that I went to bed devoting my Royal Master to all the infernal gods.

In the morning, being on guard, I mentioned what had occurred, with some chagrin, to my colonel, Lord Frederick Bentinck, who goodnaturedly told me not to take the matter to heart, as it was really of no consequence; and he added— "Depend upon it, Gronow, the prince who is a lover of novelty, will wear trousers himself before the year is out, and then you may laugh at him."

Lord Frederick proved a true prophet, for in less than a month I had the satisfaction of seeing "the finest gentleman in Europe" at a ball at Lady Cholmondeley's, dressed exactly as I had been at Lady Hertford's, when I incurred his displeasure, in black trousers and shoes; and Lord Fife, who was in attendance, upon the Prince, congratulated me upon the fact that his royal master had deigned to take example by the young Welshman.

The Prince Regent was a great believer in gas, the new form of illuminant at this time beginning to displace candles, and he was probably responsible for the first ballroom to be so lighted. When the buildings of the Royal Pavilion, Brighton, were being improved and the Banqueting and Music Rooms added (1815-1817) he arranged for gas lighting. Originally he contemplated a private gas works, but, the Brighton Gas Light & Coke Co. having come into operation in 1818, the gas was taken from the public supply and the gas holder ordered for the private works was sold to the Gas Light & Coke Co. of London. The chandeliers which still exist were specially designed and are most ornate. Some weighed over a ton and exceeded £5,000 each in cost. In October 1818 the Prince Regent and John Nash were present at the Pavilion to witness their first lighting up.

Another interesting conversion to gas was that of the Great Ballroom of the Liverpool Town Hall in 1820. A grand ball attended by 1,000 guests was given by the ex-Mayor, Sir John Tober, to celebrate the occasion. A contemporary report states "the three great chandeliers which in size, elegance and beauty are the admiration of every spectator were brilliantly lighted with gas and threw over the whole scene a radiance never before witnessed". These fine three-decker chandeliers, now converted to electricity, are still in use.

Although theatres adopted gas about 1820 and some Assembly Rooms in 1830, it was not until after 1845 that the lighting of public hall and private salons by gas became common usage. This continued until the closing years of the century when there was a gradual change-over to electricity.

*The Galop*

Another dance to come into fashion during the first third of the nineteenth century was the Galop, known at the time as the Galopade. This is possibly the simplest dance ever introduced into the ballroom. It is in a very quick 2/4 time; the partners hold somewhat as in the Waltz but both face the line of dance and advance rapidly down the room with the series of chassés varied by an occasional turning movement. Its origin is not known with certainty but according to one account it was brought into this country from Russia.

J. S. Pollock in his *La Terpsichore Moderne* (c.1830) states:

> This new and fashionable dance ... was first introduced into this country at His Majesty's Ball, St. James's Palace, on the 11th June, 1829, when the Princess Esterhazy, the Earl of Clanwilliam,

the Duke of Devonshire, and some of the foreign ministers exerted themselves in teaching its novel movements to the company, and was danced alternately with Quadrilles and Waltzing during the whole of the evening.

About 1830 it was also introduced to form the basis of that final figure of the Quadrille which was called Saint-Simonienne and it is said that this use of the Galopade helped to popularize that other turning dance, the waltz.

## Parisian Quadrilles

On programmes towards the middle of the century, particularly at popular Assemblies, we frequently find the item "Parisian Quadrille". This was simply the first set danced in the original way but without side couples, the figures being the same with the exception of the last which was as follows: Ladies chain and double L'été, finishing with galopade.

## Lancers

Although that well known variation of the Quadrille, known as the "Quadrille des Lanciers" or more popularly "Lancers" was invented very shortly after the introduction in 1815 of the Quadrille in England and was evidently danced occasionally, it does not appear to have come into favour at the very fashionable dances until considerably later in the century.

I have found it impossible to discover with certainty who was the inventor of this dance. There are two claimants and one cannot say whether one of these "borrowed" the idea from the other or if they both drew from a common unknown source. The first record I can trace is an advertisement which appeared in the *Dublin Evening Post*, on Thursday, May 1st, 1817, which ran as follows:

NEW QUADRILLES—This Day is Published by I. Willis, No. 7 Westmoreland Street, price 3/3d.

"La Dorset," "Lodoiska," "La Native," "The Lancers," with the figures in French and English as danced at the Countess of Farnham's Ball on Wednesday 9th of April 1817 at the Nobility's Assemblies and at the Rotunda. The Music by Yaniewicz and Spagnoletti. The figures by Mr. Duval.

To which is added a new Waltz by Spagnoletti, the much-admired Stop-Waltz and the National Waltz respectively dedicated by permission to the Right Honourable the Countess of Farnham—arranged for the Pianoforte, Harp or Violin.

I have in my possession a copy of a later edition of this piece of music which bears the title "The Lancers Quadrilles or Duval of Dublin's Second Set". The title page also contains a reference to the Lancers having been danced at Almack's, and from the imprint this particular edition seems to have been published by the London office of the same firm of Willis.

Duval's figures are:

1. La Dorset   (Music by Spagnoletti)
2. Lodoiska   (Music by Kreutzer)
3. La Native   (Music from The Beggar's Opera)
4. Les Grâces (Music anonymous, with the alternative of music from *The Haunted Tower*, "Pretty Maiden," by C. E. Horn).
5. Les Lanciers   (Music by Yaniewicz).

A description of the steps used is given both in French and English, and will be found on page 141 of this book. As regards the occasion on which these were danced, the *Freeman's Journal* of Dublin, April 11th, 1817, says:

FASHIONABLE INTELLIGENCE — The Countess of Farnham held a Grand Ball and Supper on Wednesday April 9th 1817, attended by—nearly 300 fashionables.

The second claimant was one Joseph Hart, who published his "Les Lanciers, a second set of Quadrilles" in 1820, by Whitaker and Co. of London. This title page sets forth "Les Lanciers, a second set of Quadrilles for the Pianoforte with entirely new figures, as danced by the nobility and gentry at Tenby in the summer of 1819. Composed and most respectfully dedicated to Lady and the Misses Beechy by Joseph Hart. London, for the Author Whitaker & Co. 75, St. Paul's Churchyard."

Hart's figures and music were as follows:

1. La Rose   (Music by Spagnoletti)
2. Lodoiska   (Music by Kreutzer)
3. La Dorset   (Music from The Beggar's Opera)
4. Les Lanciers   (Music by Yaniewicz)
5. L'Étoile (Music by Storace—"Pretty Maiden" from *The Haunted Tower*)

It will be seen that if we take the alternative tune offered by Duval for his 4th figure, the tunes used by the two claimants are the same throughout, with the order of the last two reversed. It should be noted that after a very short time Hart made his figure "Les Lanciers" the last figure instead of the fourth.

In France, though the steps more or less corresponded, the figures were given different names, i.e.

1. Les Tiroirs ou La Dorset
2. Les Lignes ou La Lodoiska
3. Les Moulinets ou La Native
4. Les Visites ou Les Grâces
5. Les Lanciers ou La Grande Chaîne.

Further research has revealed the fact that the music for all figures was either by an English composer or arranged by a foreigner whilst in England. When selected from that of a foreign composer, that composer was in England about the time of the introduction of the dance. This leads me to suspect that the dance was of English origin.

I cannot trace the origin of the name "La Dorset" for Duval's first figure. Spagnoletti, composer of the music, was a violinist who led the orchestra at that time in the King's Theatre, London. The figure "Lodoiska" undoubtedly takes its title from the musical romance of that name partly composed by Storace and partly adapted by him from Kreutzer and Cherubini, produced in 1794. Kreutzer, it will be noted, is credited with the music for this figure.

### Caledonians

I am also unable to trace the origin of another set dance— the Caledonians—but I strongly suspect that Scotland was not responsible for this dance. They were a lively set of Quadrilles, probably created at the time when Sir Walter Scott's works were so much in the public eye. The first printed description I can find occurs in *Terpsichore Moderne,* a little ballroom guide by one J. S. Pollock, published by himself at his Walworth and Newington Assembly Rooms about 1830. They certainly appeared on the programme of many old-fashioned teachers' Assemblies until the end of the nineteenth century.

### d'Alberts

The set known as the d'Alberts or Albert Quadrilles, which was danced for many years at popular Assemblies, consisted of the first figure of the Quadrilles, the second figure of the Caledonians, the third figure of The Lancers, the fourth figure of the Waltz Cotillon (half through) and the fifth figure of the Quadrilles. It was the invention of one Charles d'Albert (1809-86), a French dancing master who, after being ballet master at the King's Theatre and at Covent Garden, settled in Newcastle and was a prolific composer of popular dance tunes of the day. He must not be confused with the Charles D'Albert who was, for a number of years, secretary of the Imperial Society of Teachers of Dancing at the beginning of the present century.

It will be remembered that when the Quadrille was first introduced extremely complicated and difficult steps were used by the best dancers, and to some extent this also applied to the Lancers. After some years, however, there was a revulsion against these difficult movements; the pendulum swung in the opposite direction and Society began to "walk" the Quadrille. On this subject Cellarius, the famous teacher of dancing, in his book *Fashionable Dancing* (1847), has the following comment to make:

> The youthful dancers of the present day, who are accused so often of walking instead of dancing, are they, then, so wrong in renouncing the entrechats, the ronde de jambes and other complicated steps in use in former days, and which had the serious inconvenience of recalling to one, most imperfectly, and often most ridiculously, those which are exhibited every day on the boards of the theatre, with all the perfection of the art?

Heinrich Heine, writing from Paris in 1832, refers to "the prevalent mode of only seeming to dance, so that the figures are only executed while walking, and the feet are only moved in an indifferent and dull and almost sulky manner."

## ★ 7 ★

## THE SECOND QUARTER (1825-1850)

THE second quarter of the nineteenth century was a period of political unrest. It also witnessed the commencement of many social changes. At home the passing of the first Reform Bill heralded a more democratic form of government and the revolution caused by the invention of the steam engine led to the Industrial Revolution that was to follow. On the Continent there were two Revolutions in France: the first in 1830 when the Bourbons were displaced from the throne by Louis Philippe of the House of Orleans; the second, eighteen years later, when in 1848 the monarchy was abolished and the Second Republic formed with Louis Napoleon as President. Four years after this, in 1852, the Empire was restored and he became Napoleon III. In 1830 Belgium broke away from Holland and became a separate kingdom and about the same time Poland unsuccessfully revolted against Russia.

It is therefore not surprising to find that our social dances were passing through a period of transition. The growing popularity of the Waltz fostered by the brilliant compositions of Lanner and Strauss established in favour the "closed" couple dance as opposed to the less personal Country Dance or Quadrille and, as previously stated, the Country Dance

passed away before the turn of the century but the Quadrille
held its place though shorn of many of its embellishments.

In London the coming social changes were foreshadowed
even at Almack's. These famous Assemblies were still exclusive but it was a more tolerant and less autocratic exclusiveness. Etiquette, however, was still most carefully observed.

Though there appears to have been a certain amount of in-
difference towards dancing among the upper classes, the
popular assemblies were as well patronised as ever, and at
Cremorne the dance platform was filled every night.

In France the opposition to the Waltz was as great as in
England, and more prolonged. The Vicomte de B. Saint
Laurent wrote a pamphlet entitled *Quelques Mots sur les
Danses Modernes* which reached a fourth edition dated 1862,
in which he levelled a bitter attack on both the Waltz and
the Polka.

> In 1840 or 1841 there were danced Quadrilles, Waltzes and the
> "Grand-Père" or the Cotillion. The number of Quadrilles were
> to that of Waltzes as five to one. Very few young girls waltzed
> and a great number of married women abstained from this dance
> introduced into France by the unchaste at the time of the
> Directoire.

About seven years earlier, in 1855, Gustave Boullay in a
booklet *Reforme de la Danse des Salons*, which certainly
reached a second edition, also protested against the so-called
immorality of the Waltz and sighed for the retention of the
Contredanse or Quadrille:

> Under the First Empire, and I even believe since the First
> Republic, the Waltz was the result of international wars, brought
> to us from Germany, but it only penetrated to the aristocracy
> after a long wait in the antechamber before it was allowed into

the salon. From the beginning one saw that there was, in this intimacy between the dancer and his partner, something too familiar and one felt that this was not suitable for us.

In France one thinks more than one acts.

The Waltz came into our salons under the name of Galop . . . soon after . . . it came into the Contredanse and took possession of the final figure under the name of Saint-Simonienne. The name alone of this new figure ought to cause it to be excluded from our salons. Behind the final Galop appeared the Waltz. Scruples were soon dissipated—soon the energetic Waltz à deux temps, in which one used so much strength in treading the floor, and in holding up one's partner, was adopted by the smart set, in spite of the protests of experienced waltzers.

By the time Queen Victoria came to the Throne (1837) the opposition which it first had encountered had been overcome and the dance was firmly established, but not quite in its early form. Another round dance, the Galop, gained a considerable amount of popularity from 1830 onwards. So much so that it was even introduced temporarily into a final figure of the Quadrille. This had a great effect on the waltz and dancers began to galop to waltz music, thus introducing the rather foolishly named Valse à Deux-Temps which should, of course, have been called the Valse à Deux-Pas. In this form of the waltz the pas glissé of the galop occupied the first two beats, and the chassé the third beat.

All writers on the dance of this period agree that the Valse à Deux-Temps had entirely displaced the Valse à Trois-Temps in popularity.

As usual, there is some doubt as to where the Deux Temps originated. Coulon, the very famous French dancing master, who had settled in London and taught in Marlborough Street, wrote in 1844:

This waltz came out at the court of Vienna, whence it was

brought to us, and has become such a favourite as to have driven all other waltzes from the field.

Cellarius, perhaps the most famous French teacher of ball-room dancing of the period, whose works were translated into English and widely read in this country, writes enthusiastically about the valse à deux-temps:

> Now, I appeal to the waltzers themselves: Do they experience the same pleasure in performing a uniform circle round a room, to an equal movement, as when they spring with that fascinating vivacity which is so peculiar to the valse à deux temps; moderating or quickening their pace at pleasure, leading their lady as it pleases them, sometimes obliging her to retrograde, sometimes retiring themselves, flying from one room to another, turning to the right or to the left, varying their steps at every moment, and at last arriving at that pitch of excitement which I dare to call intoxication, without fear of contradiction by the true lovers of the waltz?

Cellarius does complain that, the actual steps of the valse à deux temps being so simple and so easy to learn, many attempt to dance it in the ball-room without having had a course of instruction in the classroom where they could have been taught how to make proper use of those very simple steps.

He draws attention to the fact that in this valse the steps must be glided, avoiding all leaps and jerks. This is of very great interest, as it seems to foreshadow the coming of the modern style of waltzing in which the steps are entirely glided.

G. Desrat in his Dictionnaire (1895), on information passed down to him from his father who, himself was a teacher, seems to attribute the origin of this style of waltzing to the Russians. It appears that in 1839 Desrat père was giving a lesson to the Baron de Nieuken, attaché at the Russian Legation, who was due to go that night to a ball given by the Count Mole, French Minister of Foreign Affairs, where he would have to dance with a number of charming Moscovites. He asked Desrat père to brush him up in the Valse à Deux Temps. The teacher was furious at this ridiculous name, but, when he saw his pupil dance, thoroughly understood what he meant and they practised it together to such good purpose that the Baron's Valse à Deux Temps became the rage.

In support of the above story it should be said that the Galop, from which this waltz is derived, is thought by some to have come from Russia. On the other hand, the known desire of the Viennese for fast dancing does seem a more probable answer to the query. At that time, the Valse à Trois Temps was supposed to be played at about forty-eight bars a minute, and we know that for a successful Deux Temps Valse the music must be faster and the time more strictly marked.

Gawlikowski, who seems to have been a fairly reliable writer on the dance in 1858, makes the interesting remark that the gentleman does not stand directly in front of the lady, as in the Valse à Trois Temps, but slightly to her right, thus foreshadowing the position adopted by dancers in the Boston of the early twentieth century. This was also pointed out by Cellarius.

A popular English guide (Warne's) published anonymously about 1860 says: "This valse has certainly held its position as the autocrat of the ballroom for many years past; and there are few valses more graceful than this when it is really well danced. Unfortunately, there are few dances which have amongst their pledged admirers such a vast assemblage of bad dancers as the Valse à Deux Temps". This last sentence re-echoes what Cellarius had said nearly twenty years earlier.

In England towards the close of the second quarter of the

century the coming to the throne in 1837 of a young Princess and the celebrations in connection with her marriage a few years later made conditions very favourable for the revival of interest in dancing among the "fashionables" of the day. The time was ripe for the advent of a new "closed" couple dance which would rival the waltz and restore the popularity of dancing.

There was considerable sympathy at the time in Western Europe for those peoples in Central Europe, notably the Poles and Czechs, who were still either partially or wholly under the dominance of foreign government, and in those countries a great revival of National feeling and culture arose. In Poland and Bohemia this took the form of a revival of traditional national songs, music and dances. Perhaps this state of affairs may account for the fact that it was one of these dances from Bohemia which captured first France and then the World—the Polka.

AN EARLY GAS-LIT BALLROOM
A Soirée at the Society of Fine Arts

THE ANCESTRAL HOME OF THE WALTZ
A Ball Masque in progress in the Redoutensaal, Vienna, in 1812

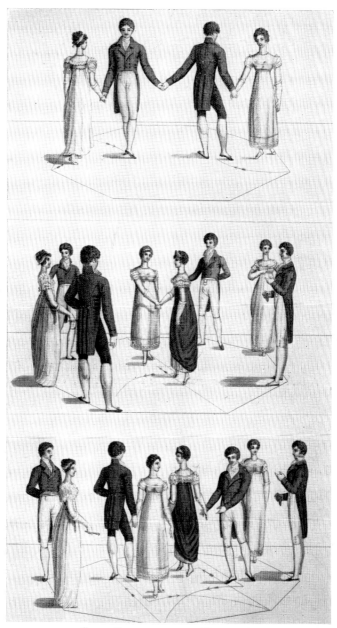

SOME FIGURES IN THE QUADRILLE
From Thomas Wilson's *Quadrille Panorama* (1822)

## ★ 8 ★

## THE POLKA CRAZE (1843)

As is the case with many other famous dances which have swept the world, there is a certain amount of mystery as regards the origin of the Polka. The popular legend is that on a Sunday afternoon in Elbeleinitz in Eastern Bohemia Josef Neruda saw a peasant girl, Anna Chadimova, extemporise this dance, singing her own accompaniment and making up the steps as she went along. He noted down the dance tune and the following Sunday Anna taught the steps to some students who took it to Prague, where it was reputedly dubbed the Polka.

If we disregard the statement that Anna herself invented the dance, there is probably a good deal of truth in this story. At this time of political unrest, as Edwin Evans points out, Societies, largely composed of students, were formed to further Czech culture and, to avoid suspicion, meetings frequently took the form of dances and country excursions. It seems highly probable that it was on one of these excursions that the dance was introduced to the townsfolk.

Dr. Arthur Michel, who appears to have made an extensive study of the subject, writing in the American *Dance Magazine* in 1944 (quoted in Anatole Chujoy's *Dance Encyclopedia*)

81

6

definitely states the Polka was a folk dance of Bohemia, probably so called out of compliment to their Polish neighbours whose revolution in 1831 produced great sympathy in Bohemia. He suggests the name may mean "the Polish Girl" and adds that etymologically the idea that it comes from "pulka" meaning a half-step is not sound.

Albert Zorn, in his *Grammar of the Art of Dancing*, written in 1887, tells us that in 1844 he "travelled from Odessa to Vienna and Paris for no other reason than to visit the most celebrated teachers of the Polka. And what did he find? Only the dance which, as a child, he had learned from his father under the name of the "Scotch Waltz" and which he had shown to his pupils in Dresden in 1835, in Christiana in 1836 and in Paris in 1837. It was not, however, until 1844 that this dance became known in Paris to those persons who understood how to advertise it."

I find Mr. Zorn a most irritating gentleman. Whenever attention is focused on some new dance he always seems to have known all about it some years before anyone else.

Curt Sachs, in his *World History of the Dance*, somewhat confirms Zorn's statement for he says:

> The polka step itself was nothing new. Its simple pattern was a combination of the old fleuret and pas de bourrée together with the so-called schottische step, with which the people of the time were familiar from the écossaise. This is why the polka, when it made its appearance in the German cities after 1830, was called the Schottische.

However, whatever may have been the origin of the Polka, I think it can be taken that its true birthplace as a fashionable ballroom dance was in the salons of Paris. It was probably first danced in this city on the stage of the Odéon in 1840 by J. Raab, a Ballet Master from Prague. The rage started in Paris in 1843 and its principal exponents were Cellarius, Laborde, Coralli and Petipa. Later on it made its appearance at the Opéra, when the performers were Coralli and Mlle. Maria.

Some idea of the excitement created by the new dance in Paris can be gained from a remark in the London *Times* of the period, when the Paris Correspondent reported : "Politics is for the moment suspended in public regard by the new and all-absorbing pursuit, the Polka."

Cellarius and Coralli, two of the most fashionable dancing masters of the period, each had his own version of this dance, and the rivalry between their supporters, if we are to believe the following story told in *La Polka Enseignée sans Maître* by Perrot and Robert, published in Paris about that time:

A great number of artists, painters, sculptors and men of letters, *les gentle-men riders les plus chocnosophes,* and a host of pretty women were present at this solemnity, at which M. Cellarius and M. Eugene Coralli were to meet face to face and polka to polka. All the votaries of the polka were on the tiptoe of expectation. Chledowski himself had composed the music for the occasion. Cellarius appeared with carefully dressed hair and glossy beard, triumphing in advance; he was surrounded by four or five experts, carefully chosen from among his best pupils. A certain anxiety was nevertheless visible in the master's face, every now and then he sprang nimbly upon the platform where the musicians were installed, and made them play over the new composition, the third polka that had been written. Then he returned in haste to his disciples, passing along the ranks haranguing them in brief, decisive phrases, animating them both by words and gestures. The great Germanicus could have done no more *pace* Tacitus.

While the master was thus engaged, Eugene Coralli, Lucien Petipa and two or three other accomplished Labordians of the opposition, preserved a scornful silence and a redoubtable calm.

At last the orchestra gave the signal of battle. The spectators made way respectfully. Cellarius led out one of his sisters, dressed in pure white like a vestal virgin, and started in full career, followed by his faithful cohort.

It was like Achilles rushing under the walls of Troy to defy Hector, and avenge the death of Patrocles; but—

> *O rage! O désespoir! O fortune ennemie,*
> *N'avait-il tant polke que pour cette infamie!*

Oh agony! No one could dance to the new tune; they required the old routine with which they had sucked the milk of Mother Polka! The performers stopped and gazed at each other in astonishment. The master in vain endeavoured to revive their courage in this extremity. "At least give us enemies we can cope with," they exclaimed. These words were an inspiration for the master. Rushing to the orchestra he threw down the traditional score before them and the complaisant musicians once more struck up the old wearisome tune, the most wearisome ever written, perhaps, with the exception of the "Bolero di Dona Lola Montez". As the familiar strains fell on their ears the Cellarians took courage; they advanced with great spirit, bringing their heels up under their coat tails in the most daring fashion, and remained masters of the field. But their triumph was not of long duration. The crowd presently parted to make way for their terrible rivals whose very first steps ensured the discomfiture of the Cellarians. The whole cohort dispersed, and the unhappy chief, his eyes darting flames, his heart full of fury, withdrew to swallow the affront as best he might.

Such was this memorable day, the events of which are so suggestive of a mock heroic poem that our very prose has been affected. Thenceforth an unquenchable hatred, direr than that of the Capulets and Montagues, reigned between the rival schools. Immediately after their defeat, the Cellarians are said to have assembled in the little Pink Boudoir and, before a statue of Hermaphrodite, to have vowed an enmity to their foes which might very well have found expression in something more than words.

An American teacher of dancing, Allan Dodsworth, writing in 1885, refers to what he obviously considered most undesirable methods used in the teaching of this dance, and says:

In Paris the rage to learn this dance became so general that Cellarius was compelled to employ many ballet-girls to assist in teaching. This method became so very popular that other places were established, where this was offered as the chief attraction, not only in Paris, but in all the large cities of Europe. Subsequently places were opened in New York, multiplying rapidly in many of our large cities. The managers of these places were not masters of motion, but simply dance teachers, and had very questionable taste in their methods. The young women willing to be employed were naturally those to whom the small amount paid was of importance; they therefore, exercised little, if any, improving influence upon those who practised with them. But being able to dance expertly, and always deeming it part of their duty to be as agreeable as possible to those who came to learn, they made the method very attractive at one time to our young men—the freedom of manners and absence of all attempt to practise the amenities of social life being to some natures very enjoyable. Small rooms were generally used, so that the crowding and squeezing of the parlour were reproduced, with surroundings not conducive to delicacy, to say the least. Many young men became very expert by this practice; but in gaining skill they lost the modesty and innocence that should accompany the pleasure.

The bad influence, unfortunately, followed them to the drawing rooms of their friends; being expert, they were desirable partners, but the methods practised in learning were communicated to their sisters and lady friends; there was, in consequence, a deterioration in the general tone of motion and manner.

The Polka craze came to England at the beginning of 1844. In April of that year Perrot and Grisi danced it on the stage of Her Majesty's Theatre, and a month later it was danced by Saint-Leon and Cerito at the same place. Of this latter display,

M. Coulon states, "It is no Polka at all, but an imitation of the celebrated Pas Styrien".

It was this M. Coulon, teacher, of Great Marlborough Street, who claims to have been one of the first to bring the dance to England. He visited Paris and learned it from Cellarius, Laborde and Coralli.

As evidence of the popularity of this new dance, Coulon reports that at a Ball given by the Duke of Wellington at Apsley House in honour of the Queen's birthday in this year (1844):

> The Polka furore rose to such a pitch as to be danced, we are told, six times during the evening. Now this will not do. In our opinion the Polka, as an addition to the various amusements of a ball, stands certainly without parallel; still it ought by no means to detract from the usual amusements by superseding all other dances. Were the spirit of Nash to rule once more over the arrangements of our ballrooms, it would, no doubt, resist such an encroachment, no matter how high the quarter in which it might originate. It would also put down any attempt to break through the following order of the dances: a quadrille, then a waltz, then again a quadrille, then a polka, and so on. By observing this order, dancers would not feel so fatigued, and the quadrille would continue to act as a pleasant relief to the waltz or polka; leaving at the same time an opportunity for gentlemen to converse with their fair partners.

The Polka craze also brought about the Tea Dance.

If we may accept a very humorous drawing in *Punch* as historical evidence, the year 1845 witnessed the introduction of Tea Dances into this country for the first time. *Punch's* reporter makes the following amusing announcement:

> Among the fashionable parties of the season we have observed the frequent announcement of a Thé Dansant, or a Dancing Tea, with which our un-aristocratic readers may not happen to

be familiar. The sort of entertainment was new even to us; for though we have heard of fêtes al fresco, or parties in the open air, which sometimes terminate in a promenade pattenique or a walk home in pattens, as well as a soirée brandy-and-water-esque, or a glass of grog at night to prevent one from catching cold; we must confess our ignorance, until lately, of a Thé Dan-sant—the nearest approach to which seems to have been the capers cut by a bull among the cups and saucers in a china-shop. Having however been honoured by an invitation from one of our aristocratic female friends to a Thé Dansant, we went a few evenings ago to an entertainment of the sort alluded to. We also took part in a set of Congou Quadrilles and danced a Bohemian Polka, together with the Hyson Waltz and Gunpower Galop.

The following description of the figures of the first set of Congou Quadrilles may prove interesting to our fair readers, who will no doubt introduce it at their soirées, as they would any other piece of eccentricity, that had novelty and fashion to recommend it.

1st Fig. LA TASSE.

First gentleman advances, and hands cup to first lady, who retires; and second gentleman does the same to second lady. Both gentlemen chassez while both ladies drink the tea, when the two ladies balancez to the two gentlemen, who take the two cups and retire.

This is delightful fooling, but it does indicate that Tea Dances were becoming fashionable in a certain section of Society. My older readers will remember that the Tango craze in 1912 brought a similar revival of interest in Thé Dansant.

In April of 1844 the *Illustrated London News* ridiculed the Polka, stating

It is a waste of time to consider this nonsense. The weathercock heads of the Parisians have been delighted always by any inno-vation, but they never imported anything more ridiculous or un-graceful than this Polka. It is a hybrid confusion of Scotch Lilt,

Irish Jig and Bohemian Waltz, and needs only to be seen once to be avoided for ever!

Nevertheless, the Polka attained such a hold upon the English public that only a month later (May 11th, 1844) this paper changed its tune and presented its readers with a full description of the dance :

> We are much gratified in being enabled to lay before our readers an accurate description of the *veritable* or Drawing-room Polka as danced at Almack's and the balls of the Nobility and Gentry in this country.
>
> La Polka having appeared before us in so many guises we determined to spare no pains to procure a true description of its dance, for which we are indebted to Mrs. James Rae who has been fortunate enough to secure the details from M. Coralli Fils, the Instructor of the young noblesse and gentry in Paris.
>
> . . . La Polka, as danced in Paris, and now adopted by us, is elegant, graceful and fascinating in the extreme; it is replete with opportunities of showing care and attention for your partner in assisting her through its performance.

Referring to the Court Balls at Buckingham Palace in the first years of Queen Victoria's reign, Mrs. Lilly Grove in her *Dancing* says :

> Quadrilles and waltzes with an occasional galop were danced throughout the evening until after Her Majesty's marriage in 1840, when the Polka appears to have been introduced and the concluding Country Dance omitted.

A reference to the *Illustrated London News* description (see page 132) will show that the Polka originally consisted of several figures, but these were quickly whittled down to the comparatively simple dance as done by our grandfathers, and which many of my older readers may remember.

The craze for the Polka was as great in London as it had been in Paris and can be likened to the Tango and Charleston crazes of more recent years. All sorts of things, from hats to puddings, were named after the new dance. The Polka stayed with us well into the 1880's as is shown by George Grossmith's famous song "See Me Dance the Polka" which was published in 1886. By the 1890's my own recollection is that about one polka would be included in an evening's programme. By the close of the century, except at Court Balls, it may be regarded as a museum piece. It was included in the State Balls at Buckingham Palace until the coming of the first World War. My last memory of the Polka is of seeing it brilliantly danced, when included as a curiosity at a ball given by the Royal Academy of Dancing in 1939, by Dame Adeline Genée and the famous Danish tenor, Lauritz Melchior.

# ★ 9 ★

## SOME MID-CENTURY DANCES
## (1843-1865)

THE mid-century, that is to say from the accession of Queen Victoria in 1837 to the death of the Prince Consort in 1861, was an exceedingly fertile time for the appearance of new dances. Unfortunately, the teachers of the period who issued printed descriptions of the steps of these dances frequently differ and it is difficult to judge which was the correct version. Moreover, these descriptions are not always clear and in many instances are difficult to follow. These old teachers have in many cases the habit of naming a number of dances which they declare were in vogue at the time. Unfortunately, in many instances this "vogue" only extended to their own assemblies and classrooms, and the dances in question were never found on smart programmes or even at popular assemblies.

It is very evident, however, that the coming of the Polka did bring about a great revival of interest in dancing, and this lasted with the fashionable world until Her Majesty went into retirement on her bereavement. The popular Assemblies which had to some extent flourished even during the dull period of William IV, continued to attract a great number of people.

Earlier in this book (page 70) I have explained the origin of that very popular variation of the Quadrille known as the Lancers, and I then pointed out how, though danced occasionally both in England and France, it never became fully recognised until the mid-century.

It was not indeed until 1850 that it was welcomed at the big society balls, when almost in a night it achieved a popularity that was to last for sixty years. The suggestion that this revival was due to the interest shewn in the dance by the Empress Eugénie is obviously impossible as that lady did not become Empress of the French until she married Napoleon III in 1853. It may indicate, however, that the set was being danced in Paris, and French ballroom guides of the period fully describe the dance, using French names for the figures.

Desrat in his *Dictionnaire* clearly states that the dance was of English origin but adds that it was introduced into France in 1868, certainly wrong but perhaps a misprint for 1848.

In England, however, the immediate cause of its revival was due, according to Mrs. Lilly Grove in her *Dancing* (Badminton series), to the enterprise of a teacher of dancing, Madame Sacré. I cannot trace the source of Mrs. Grove's story but I can see no reason to doubt its truth.

Madame Sacré was a fashionable teacher who held her classes at the old Hanover Square Rooms, in Hanover Square, which had been built by Sir John Gallini, sometime manager of Her Majesty's Opera House in the Haymarket and author of two well known books on dancing*.

---

* Giovanni-Andrea Gallini was known in this country as Sir John Gallini and I, in common with many people, used to think he was the first member of the dancing profession to be honoured by an English sovereign. The true facts are that in the course of a tour in Italy he so pleased the Pope that the latter created him a knight of the Golden Spur. On his return to England he called himself Sir John Gallini although, of course, he was not entitled to do so.

It would appear that Madame Sacré had in her possession a description of the set and that, probably having heard of the French interest, she realised its possibilities as a very attractive variation from the ordinary Quadrille. Consequently she persuaded four of her former pupils, who as débutantes occasionally visited her for what to-day we should call a "refresher" lesson, to get themselves partners and learn the dance. The four young débutantes were Lady Georgina Lygon, Lady Jane Fielding, Mdlle. Olga de Lechner (daughter of Baroness Brunow, Russian Ambassadress in England) and Miss Berkeley. After they had thoroughly mastered the intricacies of the set they danced it before their admiring friends at some of the big balls of the high season. The Lancers were very favourably received and slowly but surely won their way into popular favour both at the smart dances of the Upper Ten and the more popular gatherings; in fact by the beginning of the last quarter of the century they almost eclipsed the Quadrille as the principal square dance.

For some time after the revival of the Lancers it seems to have been the custom to use the original music but gradually other tunes were substituted to the great disgust of the anonymous author of the *Ballroom Companion* who wrote:

> We cannot consider this an improvement. The old simple melodies are peculiarly fitted to the sprightly joyous character of the dance which is more than can be said for any of the modern substitutes. When these are used, in our opinion, the Lancers loses its individuality and spirit, becoming almost like a common quadrille. We should be heartily glad to see the old tunes restored once more to the rightful supremacy.

The complaint passed unheeded for experience has shewn that a dance which can only be done to one tune can never have a long life, and the Lancers was far too popular to be allowed to die for this reason. As a matter of fact, it became customary for the music to be based on popular musical comedies, operettas and even operas of the day and Messrs. Chappell & Co., the well-known music publishers, tell me that their first publication of this nature was in 1873 when they issued a set of Lancers based on airs from Lecoq's Opera "La Fille de Madame Angot". A few years later they issued another set based on airs from Sullivan's "Trial by Jury". In the 'nineties I remember dancing to "The Shop Girl", "The Geisha", "La Poupée" and "The Savoy" (Sullivan) Lancers.

I believe the Lancers were always correctly taught in the best schools and that for a time they were correctly danced, but many did not trouble to have lessons and merely walked the set. Later on, the overwhelming popularity of the waltz encouraged those who did not know the correct steps to waltz whenever possible thus entirely spoiling the effect particularly of such a pleasant figure as "visiting". Instead of the first gentleman leading his lady to visit the side couples in a series of steps accurately fitted to the music, he made the journey in a series of waltz turns.

This gradually gave rise to those boisterous sets known at the time as the "Kitchen Lancers" in which the ladies were frequently swung off their feet in the third figure, and in the fifth after the chain the four men sometimes linked arms and in a series of side chassés rushed from one end of the room to the other, racing back just in time for the Grand Chain.

Except at the two ends of the scale, Court Balls and Popular Assemblies, the Quadrille was completely ousted by the Lancers which continued to be the most popular square dance until the close of the century. In the early years of the present century it rapidly declined and after the first World War it was almost confined to those balls featuring Old Time dances.

Following the phenomenal success of the Polka, several other dances from Eastern Europe made their appearance in the salons of Paris. From Poland came the Polonaise and the Mazurka. I cannot trace any evidence that they achieved any measure of popularity in England but they were occasionally used, and so some reference must be made to them.

The Polonaise would be more accurately described as a stately processional march in 3/4 time taken at a moderate to lively tempo. There are various accounts of its origin. According to one it was derived from a warrior's triumphant march after victory: according to another it was purely an invention of the Court introduced in 1573 at a great ball at Cracow to welcome Henry III of Anjou who had been elected King of Poland. Thus there may be some connection between the Polonaise and the old Pavan. It became customary in Poland and subsequently in other Eastern European Courts to open a ball with this dance.

I have seen an account of a Polonaise danced in Paris as early as 1830, that is even before the coming of the Polka. This was at a great ball in the Palais Royale given by the Duc d'Orléans, and was led in Hungarian costume by Rodolf Apponyi who, three years previously, had introduced a new form of Cotillon to Parisian society.

Writing in the *Dancing Times* in April 1928 that very famous Maître de Ballet, Nicolas Legat, who took a great interest in those ballroom dances derived from Eastern European folk dances, described the Polonaise as follows:

"This dance consists of a ceremonial procession to a rhythm of three beats to a bar. A chain of couples is formed, proudly moving one after the other, each gentleman leading a lady by the hand on his right. He should regard her with a smile expressive of dignified greeting, the while she returns his look with one of tenderness, yet reserved and proud. Each link of the chain should present an enraptured pair of the stronger and weaker sex.

At every third step all the couples simultaneously make a slight bend of the knee. At the conclusion of the first circuit of the hall the couples divide, the gentlemen and ladies, with a slight bow towards each other, taking different directions, but continuing to follow one another with their eyes. Thus completing half the circuit of the hall, they rejoin, greeting each other with another bow. The gentleman takes the lady's hand as before and the procession proceeds, embellished with all manner of figures of movement dependent upon the imagination and phantasy of the director of the dance. The procession ends with a mutual bow, each gentleman then conducting his lady to her seat."

The Polonaise survived for a long time in Russia, Poland and Germany and gained some popularity in the salons of Paris. In England it had a fitful existence, occasionally being used as the opening dance at a costume ball. The great Costume Ball given by Queen Victoria at Buckingham Palace in 1846 (see page 108) was opened with a Polonaise led by the Queen and the Prince Consort, who had possibly brought over the idea from Germany.

I can remember that at a Costume Ball held at the Portman Rooms as late as the 'nineties the Committee, some of whom were of Russian extraction, decided that the costume parade should take the form of a Polonaise, not at the beginning of the ball, but just before supper. At some public assemblies in this country even towards the close of the century a "Grande Promenade" of all the dancers was held. Today the Polonaise is confined to the stage and the ballet, and famous examples are to be found in "Coppelia", "Swan Lake" and "The Sleeping Beauty".

*Mazurka*

About 1845 the Mazurka became known in England. Although this dance had a considerable vogue in the fashionable salons of Paris and was in great favour at the Courts of Eastern Europe, I do not think it ever obtained any real footing in our country, though occasionally introduced as a figure in a Cotillon. It is nevertheless of considerable importance, as it exercised an undoubted influence on other dances. It is derived from a Polish folk dance from the province of Masovia, subsequently taken up by the officers of the Polish army, brought by them into the ballrooms and later introduced into Russia, Germany and France. Generally in 3/4 time, it has that peculiarity of many Polish dances of one strongly accented beat.

In Western Europe it appears to have been danced as a set with four or eight couples. Though there were certain more or less recognised movements, notably the pas de mazurka itself, it was a dance in which much extemporisation was permitted and expected.

Nicholas Legat in the article already quoted, says:

"Like the Polonaise, the Mazurka may also be embellished with a variety of figures improvised by the director of the dances."

Cellarius writing in 1847 says:

"The real dancer of the mazurka not only varies his steps, but more frequently invents them, creating new ones that belong only to himself, and which others would be wrong in copying with servility."

Coulon in 1844 likens the dance to a "Russian Cotillon", and states that it was introduced into England by the Duke of Devonshire on his return from Russia after his residence there as British ambassador.

MORE QUADRILLE FIGURES
From Thomas Wilson's *Quadrille Panorama* (1822)

ACCIDENTS IN QUADRILLE DANCING—DOS À DOS AND VIS À VIS
After engravings by Cruikshank

Today the Mazurka is confined to the stage, particularly to the ballet, and most readers will have seen the famous Mazurka in "Coppelia". Chopin composed a very great number of Mazurkas and two are used as solo dances in Fokine's Ballet, "Les Sylphides".

The Polka Mazurka appears to have been an invented dance based on a Polka danced to Mazurka music. It had a certain vogue for a time in Paris but was never very popular in England. Zorn suggests that it came originally from Russia where it was invented by the Princess Marie Nicolaewna, but he is not prepared to confirm this statement. He claims that he did see the dance in Odessa some time before it was shown in Paris.

In spite of the suggestion contained in its name that the Varsoviana was a Polish dance, it definitely originated in Paris about 1853. It was the invention of a young Spanish teacher named Désiré who is said to have launched it at the Bal Public in the Rue de la Chaussée d'Antin, and it is reputed to have been taken up by the Empress Eugénie and introduced into the programme of some balls given at the Tuilleries. One Francisco Alonso wrote the music, which was in 3/4 time with a strong accent on the first notes of the second and fourth bars. The dance was a pleasing combination of polka and mazurka step. Zorn says that it is a round dance which proceeds by means of regular turns along the line of direction to the right. It consists of two parts, each of eight measures.

Warne's *Ballroom Guide*, published in the early 1860's states:

> "This dance is seldom danced now though it formerly had a sort of ephemeral popularity. We always considered it as rather a boisterous sort of performance, and more suitable for the casino than the private ballroom."

7

Today the Varsoviana is included in the syllabus of the "Victorian and Sequence Dance" junior section of the Imperial Society of Teachers of Dancing. In his book *Old Time and Novelty Dances*, Major Cecil Taylor, the late President of the Imperial Society and the originator of the "Victoria and Sequence Dance" branch, gives a very clear description of how he taught this dance. As Major Taylor learned this from his father who would be a contemporary of the original introducer I am inclined to attach considerable weight to his description.

Mention should here be made of a dance which was occasionally seen in England about 1845. This was the Cellarius or Mazurka Waltz, the invention of the well-known Parisian dancing master who has already been referred to. In his book *The Drawing Room Dances*, Cellarius writes:

> "The Mazurka-waltz may be danced to all the airs of the mazurka, only the orchestra must take a more animated movement, and well emphasize the attack of every bar."

Although generally admitted to be a most graceful dance, the Cellarius never achieved any popularity, partly owing to the difficulty of its steps and partly due to the temporary demand for rapid whirling dances such as the polka.

About 1845 another dance from Eastern Europe is said to have claimed a passing popularity in the ballrooms of Paris and to a lesser degree in those of London. This was the Redowa, which came from Bohemia. In the country of its origin the dance appears to have had two forms; the one in 3/4 or 3/8 time suggestive of a waltz, the other in 2/4 time and somewhat in the nature of a polka. It was the former which became generally adopted in Western Europe. There was at first a preliminary movement known as "the Pursuit" in which the gentleman propelled his partner, she going backwards, down the room, or alternatively going backwards himself with his partner following him.

The descriptions of this dance by contemporary writers are most confusing and exceedingly difficult to follow. Cellarius himself, writing in 1847, suggests that already it was more talked about than danced, and English writers, a few years later, comment that it was seldom seen. Nevertheless, this dance would appear to have had a considerable influence on dancing, particularly on the valse à deux temps, and of that American outcome of the last named known as the Boston.

As late as 1894 or 1895 I can clearly remember being present at a popular assembly in London when the Redowa was announced, but only about three veteran couples, who referred to the dance with great awe and respect, were able to perform it.

Desrat writing about that time referred to it as a very graceful dance which had had some vogue in the mid-century but had long been abandoned, although an attempt was made to revive it under the name of Boston—but in vain.

An American writer, Allan Dodsworth, in his *Dancing and its Relations to Education and Social Life* (New York, 1885) says:

"Our beautiful waltz of today is a subdued redowa. Those who failed in those days, finding this redowa beyond their power of accomplishment, modified it to the hop waltz, as those who fail now modify the waltz to what is called the Boston; both of the modifications are childish forms of waltzing, scarcely worthy of adults."

About 1827 a new form of Cotillon was introduced into the fashionable balls in Paris by the Count Rodolph Apponyi, cousin of the Austrian ambassador. And as one of the great leaders of society in those days, the Duchesse de Berry, took it up, it became very popular and was danced even at the Court Balls.

For this new form of Cotillon, which partook rather of the nature of a dancing game than a serious dance, the company sat in couples on chairs round the room, the gentlemen always having their partners on their right. At the head of the room sat the leader of the Cotillon with his partner, and the figures and evolutions which the company had to do were entirely at his whim. Sometimes they were based on a waltz, sometimes on the polka or the mazurka, and frequently these dances were intermingled. It will thus be seen how important it was that the leader should be not only a good dancer, but have a fertile imagination, as upon him rested the success of the Cotillon.

Cellarius in his book *The Drawing Room Dances* described no fewer than eighty-three possible Cotillons, and Desrat in his *Le Cotillon* gives eighty-nine including many which differ from those given by the former writer.

The Cotillon achieved some amount of popularity at fashionable balls in London, particularly as the final dance of the evening.

The Honourable Mrs. Armytage writing in Mrs. Lilly Grove's *Dancing* says:

"Perhaps one of the most noticeable cotillons ever danced was at the famous ball given by the Brigade of Guards to the Prince and Princess of Wales on June 26th, 1863 . . . The second great International Exhibition was over, and the vast building standing empty in Cromwell Road was secured for the entertainment. . . . The immense galleries were transformed into a series of magnificent reception rooms, one of the largest was devoted to dancing, and on this occasion Mr. Godfrey, the well-known bandmaster, composed his most popular waltz, "The Guards", which was the delight of ball-goers for some years. Notwithstanding the size of the ballroom, it was densely crowded till a very late (or early) hour, and a Cotillon begun after two o'clock had not finished till the clock struck five. The numbers who had stayed to join it may be estimated by the fact that chairs all round this enormous room were required to seat the dancers."

In the early days of the Cotillon simple accessories were used, such as cushions, mirrors, spare chairs or anything else that might be at hand. Later on it became customary to present the ladies with flowers, but by degrees the presents grew more extravagant. Several firms specialised in the making of suitable gifts by which hostesses bribed their guests to come to their balls. I have in my possession a small book *Le Cotillon, Manuel de la Danse* published in Paris by Ouachée in the closing years of the nineteenth century which gives suggestions for a number of Cotillon figures which at that late period were almost entirely based on the waltz. The book, however, is really an advertisement for an establishment known as "Au Paradis des Enfants", 156 Rue de Rivoli, Paris, and the final twenty-eight pages are devoted to an illustrated price list of the various accessories required for these Cotillons. These range in price and variety from paper flags of all the nations at 2·50 francs a dozen to silk sashes at 72 francs a dozen, and miniature billiard tables and a game "The Greasy Pole" costing some hundreds of francs.

Although the Cotillon ceased to be danced in England sometime before the close of the century, the custom of giving presents was, strange to say, revived between the two world wars, particularly at smart hotels and dance clubs on Gala Nights.

In Paris, the Cotillon lingered into the twentieth century and I had the pleasure on several occasions of meeting M. André de Fouquières, the arbiter of fashion and good taste in Parisian ballrooms and the leader of any Cotillon that might be held. It was de Fouquières, it may be remembered, who played a very big part in the taming of the Argentine Tango to make it a dance fit for the best Parisian society.

Another dance which had a considerable vogue in England, particularly at popular and upper middle class assemblies during the mid-century, was the Schottische. This was first danced in England about 1848. It was a round dance with music somewhat similar to that of the Polka, but played slower. It must not be confused with the Écossaise (see page 53).

About this dance Zorn writes:

> "In the year 1850 there appeared in all parts of Europe the 'Schottische', a round dance which had, as early as 1844, been executed in Bavaria under the name 'Rheinlaender', and in the Rhenish countries it was known as the 'Bavarian Polka'. The music, which is in 2-4 measure, is rendered very slowly, with the effect of 4-4 time."

Zorn like all other writers cannot explain why this dance was called the Schottishche, which is the German spelling of the word Scottish. He does make the interesting remark that "If, as sometimes happens, the guests desire a Rheinlaender or a Schottische, and the musicians have no music for either of these dances, any Polka played in half-time will answer the purpose."

Routledge's Ballroom Guide, published about 1860, says that "although its name Schottische would seem to imply that it came from Scotland, there is no doubt that it is essentially German alike in character and in music."

On the other hand, the anonymous author of Warne's Ballroom Guide, published about the same time, is somewhat scoffy about this dance and writes: "This is, if possible, danced less than the Polka in the upper circles. It is deemed to be irretrievably vulgar. With children and young persons it is, however, still a favourite."

In the last two decades of the century the Schottische was very seldom danced, but it was found occasionally on the programmes of popular assemblies.

Mr. Douglas Kennedy, the Director of the English Folk Dance and Song Society, has sent me the following interesting remarks on the Schottische:

> The Schottische was invented by the dancing master Markowski nearly a hundred years after the appearance of the Écossaise. This couple dance was given the rhythm of the Strathspey and may have been from the first danced to Scottish airs, but its name and association with Scotland clearly exercised a great appeal. It does not seem to have had any vogue in Paris and it is not mentioned by Cellarius in his book "La Danse des Salons" (1847). But it found favour in North Britain, where the rhythm (now styled Schottische) was long familiar, and not only in Scotland. When the invented Schottische couple dance reached the Border it found a ready soil in which to root, for there the reels and hornpipes had that "snap" which is now regarded as the distinctive feature of Scottish traditional dance music. The Keel Row is a Tyneside song, and that is in Schottische time. A "broken" hornpipe played with snap can be made indistinguishable from a Schottische.
>
> It was no doubt the appreciation of the exciting effect of the Scottish snap which prompted the Polish dancing master to his invention. The snap itself may well have grown out of the technique of playing dance music on the bagpipes, which are sounded by a stream of air kept under pressure and released only in "staccato" spurts.

Another dance to which I feel a brief reference should be made is the Circassian Circle of which we occasionally hear. Coulon, who has already been quoted, gives perhaps the best description when he says this is a dance of modern introduction into England. All the company may join in it, for which reason it is well adapted as a concluding dance. The couples are arranged in a circle round the room, the ladies on the right hand of the gentlemen: the first and second couple commence the figure facing each other; at the conclusion the first couple with the fourth, and the second with the third couple recommence the figure and so on until they go completely round the circle meeting at the place from whence they first started: the dance is then concluded. The figures to this dance may be taken either from the country dance, or from the quadrille: the waltz figures may also be introduced with advantage. We do hear of the temporary popularity about 1860 of "La Tempête" which was brought from Paris and in the words of an anonymous *Ballroom Guide* of the period:

> speedily became a favourite and for several seasons was much danced in London and the Provinces. It unites the cheerfulness of the quadrille with the sociability of the Country Dance; and when its lively figures are correctly performed is both amusing and animated.

La Tempête is also mentioned and described in *How to Dance,* probably by W. Lamb and published about 1895.

# ★ IO ★

## SOME MID-CENTURY PROGRAMMES —ROYAL AND POPULAR

By the time Queen Victoria came to the Throne the Quadrille was firmly established as the ceremonial Court dance, and the State Balls, held at Buckingham Palace, always began with a set of Quadrilles in which the Queen would dance with her most important guest.

It is interesting to place on record that the Palace was equipped for gas when it was reconditioned for Queen Victoria to take up her residence in 1837-8. The then ballroom was lit in 1845 with 540 gas lights on the Albo-Carbon principle. Each of these would be about twenty candle power, so the whole installation would exceed 10,000 candle power. The present ballroom was built in 1856 and was gas-lit from the start. As can be imagined, the lighting of the palace gave the cachet to gas lighting of all important indoor rooms, in public halls and large private houses.

In the early years of the reign the ball would conclude with a Country Dance, but after her marriage to Prince Albert the last named dance was omitted and the Polka inserted in the programme.

The following account of a State Ball held in the mid 40's is extracted from periodicals of the time:

> There was a very large Company which included a number of Scottish noblemen, particularly the Marquis of Douglas and Lord Glenlyon, and gentlemen wearing Highland costume.
>
> At 10 o'clock the Queen and Prince Albert and the Royal Party who had assembled in the Yellow Room entered the Ballroom where at the south end, in a gallery, M. Collinet and a band of twenty-five specially chosen musicians were in attendance. Her Majesty with H.S.H. Prince Edward of Saxe-Weimar as partner opened the ball in a set of quadrilles facing Prince Albert who danced with Countess Dietrichsen, the Austrian Ambassadress. Other quadrilles and waltzes followed and at 11 o'clock the Queen passed into the Throne Room where Julien and Konig's Band played a quadrille from "Kaya ou l'Amour voyageur". A quadrille with music from the ballet *Eoline* followed. Waltzes, a Stop Polka and a Bohemian Polka were also played. Supper was served at midnight.
>
> After supper Her Majesty's Piper Mr. Mackay was in attendance to play a Highland Reel and a Reel of Tulloch. More quadrilles and waltzes followed and Her Majesty retired at a quarter to two.

During the remainder of the century the programme at all State Balls was made up of Quadrilles and Waltzes with two or three Polkas and sometimes a Galop to finish. The Lancers were occasionally introduced in place of one of the Quadrilles. How standardised this programme became will be seen when it is pointed out that, as late as 1911, the first State Ball of the reign of George V consisted of three Quadrilles, fifteen Waltzes, three Polkas and a Galop.

A writer who was present at one of these balls in the 'nineties when Queen Victoria was living in retirement and the Prince of Wales took her place, says:

No bow or curtsey is made at the commencement, as was formerly done in olden days in Quadrilles, but the first time of meeting in the course of the figure the ladies make a slight curtsey to the Prince or Princess in passing. The movement of "the advance and retire" is rarely made, a retreat of one step being sufficient, when the dancer proceeds to the opposite place in the usual way.

Here, as a matter of curiosity, is given the full programme including the music of a State Ball at Buckingham Palace held shortly before the Boer War. The music was played by a Viennese Orchestra and it will be noted that it was almost entirely of German origin.

| 1. | Quadrille | "Methusalem" | Strauss |
| 2. | Waltz | "Schneeballen" | Zichrer |
| 3. | Polka | "Die Brieftaube" | Kral |
| 4. | Quadrille | "Paris Leben" | Offenbach |
| 5. | Waltz | "Sourire d'Avril" | Depret |
| 6. | Polka | "Violetta" | Strauss |
| 7. | Quadrille | "Boccaccio" | Suppé |
| 8. | Waltz | "Gross Wien" | Strauss |
| 9. | Polka | "Schneidig" | Zichrer |
| 10. | Quadrille | "Zigeunerbaron" | Strauss |
| 11. | Waltz | "Ueber den Wellen" | Rosas |
| 12. | Polka | "Die Schöne Wienerin" | Drescher |
| 13. | Waltz | "Runaway Girl" | Caryll |
| 14. | Polka | "Aus Lieb zu ihr" | Strauss |
| 15. | Waltz | "Traum der Liebe" | Fahrbach |
| 16. | Galop | "Wien über Alles" | Strauss |

In addition to what may be called the Official State Balls, the Queen who was very fond of dancing and no mean performer, held a number of Costume Balls in the early years of her reign. There is a well-known lithograph showing such a ball at Buckingham Palace on June the 13th, 1851, when the guests wore costumes of the time of Charles II. The moment depicted by the artist (Eugene Lami) was the presentation of those taking part in the English, Scottish, French and Spanish Quadrilles.

Another important Costume Ball of the mid-century has been described as follows:

> Her Majesty gave one of the most magnificent Balls ever seen at the Palace. This was a "Historical Costume Ball" at which the guests wore dress of the 1740-1750 period—that is of one hundred years earlier. The Queen did not impersonate any particular person but wore the dress of a Queen of England of that time. Prince Albert wore an elaborate embroidered costume of a civilian of the same period.
>
> The Ball was opened with a Polonaise led by the Queen and Prince Albert through all the rooms, the various Bands playing, of course, the same tune which had been specially composed by Musard for the occasion. The assembled guests then passed in procession before Her Majesty and the Royal party. For this Ball the Minuet was revived and both the Menuet de la Cour and the Menuet d'Exaudet were danced, presumably by those who had been specially coached for the occasion. Special music for a set of quadrilles was composed by Musard called "Quadrille de 1845 de la Cour d'Angleterre, ou Souvenir de 1740". Musard, Weippert and Collinet led the dance bands and the Ball concluded with Sir Roger de Coverley danced in the Picture Gallery.

At the fashionable dances, other than those at Court, during the mid-century the quadrille, the waltz and the polka were undoubtedly the favoured items. After 1850 the Lancers became popular and gradually took the place of the Quadrille. At some County and Hunt Balls an occasional Country Dance may have lingered, and at certain very smart houses in the

Metropolis a Cotillon might be introduced, and this in its turn might contain figures in which the Mazurka or the Polka Mazurka were used.

There were no Palais de Danse in those days. Nevertheless in the mid century there were in London one or two very large popular Assembly Rooms which can be compared with the modern Palais. There was for instance Laurent's Casino on the site of what afterwards became Gatti's Adelaide Gallery in the Strand. This opened at seven o'clock, closed at half past eleven, and the admission charge was one shilling. Here is a typical programme of 1848:

| | | | |
|---|---|---|---|
| 1. | Quadrille (First Set) | "Robert Bruce" | Musard |
| 2. | Polka | "Souvenir de l'Hippodrome" | Fessy |
| 3. | Valse | "Pas des Fleurs" | Maretzek |
| 4. | Parisian Quadrille | "Le Comte de Carmagnola" | Bosisio |
| 5. | Cellarius Valse | "New National Mazurkas" | Sapinsky |
| 6. | Parisian Quadrille | "Don Pasquale" | Tolbecque |
| 7. | Polka | "Eclipse" | Koenig |
| 8. | Valse | "Le Romantique" | Lanner |
| 9. | Parisian Quadrille | "Nino" | Coote |
| 10. | Polka | "Polka d'Amour" | Wallenstein |
| 11. | Parisian Quadrille | "Les Fêtes du Château d'Eu" | Musard |
| 12. | Polka | "Les Amazones" | Val Morris |

Somewhat similar places were the New Argyll Rooms in Windmill Street on the site of the old Trocadero Music Hall and the modern Trocadero Restaurant, and the Casino de Venise in High Holborn. The last named, like some of our modern dance halls, was a swimming bath in summer. Old engravings of these two Rooms show that the men took the floor still wearing their hats.

Two other mid-century popular programmes may be quoted:

| AMICABLE ASSEMBLY | Mr. HENRY'S BALL |
| Mitchell's Rooms | "Mott's" |
| March 5th, 1846 | 1847 |

| | | | |
|---|---|---|---|
| 1. | Waltz Cotillion | 1. | Quadrille (Pastorale) |
| 2. | Lancers | 2. | Lancers |
| 3. | Spanish Dance | 3. | Spanish Dance |
| 4. | First Set | 4. | Quadrille (Trenis) |
| 5. | Polka, Cotillion and Polka | 5. | Polka |
| 6. | Caledonians | 6. | Caledonians |
| 7. | Cellarius | 7. | Cellarius Waltz |
| 8. | First Set and Post Horn Galop | 8. | Quadrille (Pastorale) |
| | | 9. | Redowa Waltz |
| | | 10. | Polka |
| 9. | First Set | 11. | Sir Roger |
| 10. | Spanish Dance and Circle | 12. | Quadrille (Trenise) |
| 11. | Lancers | 13. | Polka |
| 12. | Polka Cotillion and Polka | 14. | Waltz |
| 13. | Hussars | 15. | Quadrille (Pastorale) |
| 14. | Cellarius | 16. | Polka |
| 15 | Caledonians | 17. | Quadrille (Trenise) |
| 16. | Waltz Cotillion and Circle | 18. | Circular Waltz and Post Horn Galop |
| 17. | First Set | 19. | Quadrille (Pastorale) |
| 18. | Roger de Coverley | 20. | Polka |
| | | 21. | Quadrille (Pastorale) |

These two programmes indicate that the waltz was not in great demand at this type of Assembly and that the quadrille was by far the most popular dance. The words "First Set" in the first programme refer, of course, to the first set of Quadrilles, that is the original one as introduced at Almack's thirty-one years previously. In the Mott's programme the words "Pastorale" (an erroneous spelling of Pastourelle) and "Trenise" probably indicate which of those alternate figures was to be used (see page 59).

I am unable to trace the locality of Mitchell's but Mott's, also known as the Portland Rooms, was in Foley Street. I frequently danced here myself in the late 'nineties at the Portland Dances, a series organised by a Mr. Robinson whose patrons came mostly from the big drapery houses of Oxford Street, such as Peter Robinson, Marshall and Snelgrove, Jay's and John Lewis. It was here that I saw my first waltz competition, judged by Mr. Robinson himself, and it was here that I saw Mr. H. R. Johnson's merry square dance "Carnival" which in recent years, at my suggestion, Mr. Sydney Thompson has so successfully revived.

Until Mott's came to an end about 1868, it seems to have played quite an important role in the night life of London and had attracted many of the "smart set" of those days. It was a period when the young bucks of the town took a great delight in practical jokes and on one occasion Mott's was the scene of a very unpleasant one. It is said that the Marquess of Hastings and two friends one evening, having secured by some means or other a sack of sewer rats, smuggled them into the building. As the company was entering the ballroom after supper they cut off the gas at the meter and let the rats loose on the ballroom floor, making their escape during the confusion which followed*.

---

* This account of this very unpleasant practical joke is extracted from a remarkable little volume by W. H. Holden entitled *They Startled Grandfather*. This book published in 1930 is full of the most interesting accounts of the night-haunts of London which found favour in Victorian days, from Cremorne to the New Argyll Rooms and the Holborn Casino.

*A note on Women's Dress.*

By the end of the first quarter of the century women's dress had lost the classical lines of the early years referred to on page 66. About 1827 in Paris petticoats were stuck out with whalebone, a mode which did not affect England until quite twenty years later. In the early Victorian years women's dress was distinguished by starched and voluminous petticoats which increased in volume during the 'forties. In the later years a type of horsehair stuffing known in France as "crin" was used to hold them out but it was not until after 1850 that the crinoline, as we call the petticoat held out by whalebone, wire or cane, came into use in this country. In some form or other it was fashionable until towards the end of the 'sixties, at first shaped like a dome, but afterwards flattened in front with the bulk of the garment projecting backwards. A well-known authority stated that an examination of thousands of contemporary photographs reveals that the majority of English women never wore the huge "cage" shown in fashion plates of the day.

THE GALOP

From a music cover drawn by J. Brandard (1840) for *The Argyll Galop*
by Henri Laurent, dedicated to The Patrons of the Argyll Rooms and
published by Boosey & Sons

THE POLKA
Sketches by Geoffroy
showing two Varia-
tions described by
Eugene Coralli in his
*La Polka*

## ★ II ★

## THE SECOND HALF (1865-1900)

THE Prince Consort died in December 1861 and Queen Victoria went into retirement and passed her days either in the Isle of Wight at Osborne House, in Scotland at Balmoral or at Windsor Castle.

The mid-century dancing enthusiasm amongst the aristocracy in England, which followed the coming of the Polka and lasted for a considerable number of years, began to wane, and in a year or so died away altogether. A spirit of lethargy pervaded the fashionable ballrooms of this country. With the exception of the Barn Dance in 1888 and for one short season only the Washington Post in 1894, Society took no interest in any new dance. With the outbreak of the Boer War in the closing years of the reign, dancing in the fashionable world was at its lowest ebb, and it was even considered "bad form" for a man to dance too well.

During this period our programmes included Lancers, occasional Quadrilles and Polkas, perhaps a Galop and innumerable Waltzes.

From about 1865 onward the story of the waltz is exceedingly involved and difficult to follow. I am inclined to believe that at popular assemblies the old Trois Temps Valse never lost its place and that the only change in its execution was the abolition of any suggestion of a hop. At the more aristocratic dances, and this it must be remembered was a period when social distinctions were very clearly marked, the Deux Temps Valse was still very much in evidence, though there were not wanting signs of a return of the fast Trois Temps.

It was then that that younger nation, the United States of America, after its troubles of the Civil War were over, took a hand in the game and, out of the various forms of waltzing which had reached them, evolved new forms—particularly that known as the Boston.

Allan Dodsworth, who was born at Sheffield in England in 1817, was taken to New York in 1826 and spent the rest of his life in America. He opened his first Academy in New York in 1842 and became recognised as one of the most fashionable teachers of ballroom dancing in the States. In an early book published in New York about 1876 on the subject of the Boston, he writes:

> The origin of this dance has been, and still is, a frequent subject of discussion. I incline to the belief that it is not an invention, but a growth springing out of a natural desire in our young people for a change.
>
> We had been hopping in the "hop Waltz", jumping in the quick "redowa" for a number of years; had allowed those who were so inclined free licence to tear about in the galop, until this desire for a change to a more composed and gentle style became general. This manifested itself in subduing the "redowa" and, the progress continuing, resulted in the present "Boston".
>
> Let us be thankful for the good taste that has brought about so desirable a change ... I value the present opportunity of observing this dance from its beginning, and have noticed how gradually the good taste of our young people has modified what was at first a truly ungraceful motion, until now it approaches that beautiful old-fashioned dance, the Spanish Waltz. In fact,

our modern Boston, with the dipping motion omitted, is precisely that old-fashioned waltz, and is so named by many at the present time. I felt that in its first stage, and during the transition period, I could not recommend it to my pupils; but in its present form I feel real pleasure in describing it as the latest and best.

Some of the more eccentric versions of the earlier American Bostons appear to have reached London, if we are to believe a cartoon appearing in a contemporary issue of *Punch*. This depicts a number of fashionable people dancing an imaginary version of the waltz, the "Ratcliffe High Kick" and the caption reads:

What our Waltzing is coming to:

*Distinguished Foreigner:* "Voulez-vous me faire l'honneur de danser cette valse avec moi, Mees Matilde?"

*Miss Matilde* (an accomplished waltzer): "Avec plaisir, Monsieur. Quelle est votre forme: le 'Lurch de Liverpool', le 'Dip de Boston', ou le 'Kick de Ratcliffe Highway'?"

As a matter of fact the best American Boston, as introduced to the American Colony in Paris and known in France as the "Valse Boston", was a smooth delightful dance of a skating nature. It had not a great vogue in London.

By the time the present writer was old enough to recognise what was happening in the ballroom, that is to say, about 1889, the Trois Temps Valse played at a considerable speed was being danced everywhere except at the popular assemblies, where a somewhat similar waltz, but at not more than forty-eight bars a minute, was danced.

It must be admitted that in those days at smart subscription dances, such as the Hunt and County Balls, these fast waltzes which filled a large percentage of every programme were very indifferently danced.

At some popular assemblies dancers thought it wrong to touch the floor with the heels in the course of the waltz, and I have seen a competition in which egg-shells were attached to the heels of the waltzers and the winner was the couple which kept these shells intact the longest.

In the last decade of the century, when class distinctions were very clearly marked, the population from a dancing point of view could be divided into three groups—(1) the Aristocracy consisting of the Court Circle, the Nobility and the Landed Gentry, (2) the Upper Middle Class which included successful business men, and their families, Doctors, Barristers, Solicitors and other professional men, Members of the Stock Exchange, and Officers of the Navy and Army below the highest ranks, and finally (3) the Lower Middle Classes. There were no hard and fast dividing lines between these classes which merged into one another.

It was the aristocracy who danced so indifferently, though they were afforded countless opportunities to display their powers. There were innumerable Hunt and County Balls which were extremely exclusive and for which the great ladies of the land filled their houses with large and most aristocratic house parties and these great ladies themselves gave a number of private dances on a very lavish scale. In 1895 for instance the Marchioness of Salisbury gave a magnificent ball at Hatfield House to some 700 guests including Prince and Princess Christian of Schleswig-Holstein, and a host of notabilities of the day. There was dancing in the Winter Dining Room (Austin Sparke's Band) and the Long Gallery (Band of the Herts Militia) and it is of particular interest to note that these two ballrooms were lighted by electricity. Special late trains were run to King's Cross for the benefit of the visitors.

Numbers of Subscription Dances in aid of Charity were held at which there was a mingling of the two top classes. Favoured places for these were the Suffolk Street Galleries, the Galleries of the Royal Institute of Painters in Water Colours in Piccadilly, one or two of the leading hotels and occasionally the Great Hall of the Inns of Court in the Temple.

A far higher standard of dancing was to be found at the Football, Cricket, Tennis Clubs and other Subscription balls organised by the Upper Middle Classes, though even here with a few exceptions the standard was not very high. About these dances I once wrote fifty years later (1946) in an article "Looking Backward" which appeared in the programme of a big ball at the Royal Albert Hall organised by the *News Chronicle:*

> I wonder how many of you who are in the Albert Hall to-night can carry their memories of the ballroom back to the last decade of the nineteenth century—the closing years of the Victorian Era—when dancing was somewhat in the doldrums? The waltz was then supreme: the genuine trois temps, turning waltz, into which the ultra-smart introduced a suspicion of a hop and when giddy shuffled their partners backwards on a perilous journey down the room. The strains of "Mandalay", "The Garden of Sleep," "The Eton Boating Song" and "Whisper and I shall Hear" filled every ballroom.
>
> Those were the days of wallflowers and chaperons, of "May I have the pleasure?" and other old-world courtesies of programmes and pencils, of pumps and high stiff collars, of the coveted supper-dance with its sit-down supper, and of the cry of hard-worked stewards wearing big rosettes "One couple wanted here" as the Lancers were formed. Yes. We danced the Lancers then, but very seldom in the text-book version.

Tickets for these Subscription Dances were 7/6d., 10/6d. or 12/6d., but in the case of very smart charity dances the prices were higher. A sit-down hot supper was nearly always served (not in the ballroom), there were running buffet refreshments and, after the last dance, generally either John Peel or the Posthorn Galop, a cup of hot soup was always served.

About this time, notably in Hampstead, Blackheath and Richmond, certain Series of Dances were organised at which some excellent waltzing was to be seen and toward the close of the century the Saturday Supper Club dances at the Grafton Galleries set the fashion for some years.

About 1888 a new dance which had been known in America for some years arrived in this country and was taken up by all grades of Society. This was the Military Schottische or Barn Dance. Like the Schottische which had been danced in this country in the mid-century, this consisted of two parts each of two bars. In the first the couple, side by side, advanced along the line of dance. In the second they did a complete waltz turn. I have never discovered who was the inventor.

This Military Schottische, to give the dance its correct title, was first done to a tune "Dancing in the Barn", hence it was more generally known in this country as the Barn Dance. Dancers found that its steps exactly fitted the tune of the famous Pas de Quatre by Meyer Lutz, then being danced at the old Gaiety Theatre in the burlesque "Faust Up To Date" by Florence Levey, Lillian Price, Maud Wilmott and Eva Greville and so, for a time, regardless of sense, it was programmed, especially at some of the very smart dances as "Pas de Quatre".

If we except the State Balls I think the Barn Dance was to be found on every programme for a number of years, certainly right through the first decade of the twentieth century. The Barn Dance seen at many Old-Time Dances today, which includes a retrograde movement not in the original, is generally known as the progressive Barn Dance and includes a change of partners.

It is now necessary to take a glimpse at what was happening in the ballroom of the United States where the great changes in our social dancing which took place in the first quarter of the twentieth century were already being foreshadowed. To do this, I cannot do better than quote the picture described by Sylvia Dannett and Frank Rachel in the book *Down Memory Lane* specially written by them for Arthur Murray, and I do so with the permission of the last named:

> John Philip Sousa first came out with The Washington Post March in 1891 and the music caught on immediately. It was lively and different with a new kind of beat, and the fickle public cast aside the old quadrilles and glides and reels in favour of a new style of dancing.
>
> The two-step remained the vogue for a long time because of the ninety-odd marches Sousa wrote for it in rapid succession.
>
> It was a simple dance, not much more than a double-quick march, with a skip in each step, done as rapidly as a couple could go forward, backward, and turn.

I do not think the two-step appeared on our programmes until the commencement of the new century, but an extraordinary frolic known as the Washington Post was danced everywhere for one season about 1894. Who arranged this particular sequence, I do not know, but it was curious insomuch as the gentleman stood behind, but slightly to the left of his partner, who raised her hands above her shoulders to take those of the man. As these were the days when dresses were long, it always appeared to me that the man's chief endeavour was to avoid hopping on his partner's frock. Now back to *Down Memory Lane:*

The Cake Walk came into vogue around eighteen-eighty in the South. It originated in Florida where, it is said, the Negroes got the idea from the war dances of the Seminole Indians. These consisted of wild and hilarious jumping and gyrating, alternating with slow processions in which the dancers walked solemnly in couples.

The idea grew, and style in walking came to be practised among the Negroes as an art. There were classes for the sole purpose of teaching it, and the simple feat of promenading in a dignified manner developed into the cake walk. Prizes were given to the best performers—first, ice cream and chocolates; later on, huge decorated cakes. At the end the winner cut the cake and shared it with the other dancers. This custom, according to a reliable source, gave rise to the expression: "That takes the cake."

When Florida became a fashionable winter resort, the Negroes began to dress in a special style for the performances—the men in long-tailed coats with high collars, the women in fluffy white gowns with bouquets of flowers. From Florida the cake walk spread to Georgia, the Carolinas, and Virginia, until it reached New York, where the Negroes organized clubs and gave champion belts to the best walkers, and diamond rings to women.

The Cake Walk gained a certain amount of popularity among some sections of the public in England, particularly in the Lancashire district, at the end of the nineteenth and beginning of the twentieth century. It is, however, most important, as it gives an inkling of the coming of Rag-Time.

At popular Teachers' Assemblies, often known as "shilling hops", during the closing years of the nineteenth century the favourite dances were the waltz (generally played rather slowly), the barn dance, the quadrille, the lancers, the d'Alberts, the Caledonians, Schottische and the waltz cotillon. Occasionally—I write from personal experience—we had the Berlin Polka, the Redowa, the Circassian Circle and a somewhat involved set dance which I never mastered, the Prince Imperial's.

Among the leading Assemblies of this nature were those conducted by Mr. Piaggio at his rooms in Winsley Street near Oxford Circus. Sometimes, notably on St. Patrick's Day, he held an enormous ball at the Portman Rooms in Baker Street when nearly 2,000 people danced till five o'clock in the morning. Piaggio also had a popular Hall, the Marine Palace at Margate, but this was washed away by a great storm one winter, and the grand piano was discovered at Nayland Rock.

Mr. H. R. Johnson held assemblies at the Holborn Town Hall and Mr. Arnold at his Albert Rooms at the back of the present Scala Theatre. Mr. Sydney Bishop held his dances either at the Kilburn Athenaeum or on his own premises in Quex Road, where Miss Phyllis Bedells now holds her ballet classes.

Assemblies of a distinctly higher class were held three times a week during the season at the Cavendish Rooms in Mortimer Street, a very attractive suite owned by Mr. Edward Humphrey, father of Mr. Walter Humphrey, the inventor of a number of dances. It was Mr. Humphrey who, in 1892, started a small monthly publication as a "house-organ" for his Rooms entitled *Dancing Times*, a name which I subsequently purchased from his son.

In 1892 the British Association of Teachers of Dancing was founded by a number of popular teachers; consequently this is today the oldest of all the teaching associations in this country. On the other side of the Atlantic, however, the American Society of Teachers of Dancing was organised in 1879, incorporated in 1883 and merged in 1926 into the Dancing Masters of America.

The British Association held a competition each year to discover a new sequence dance, and in the closing year of the century this competition indirectly gave us that most famous of all sequence dances, the Veleta.

The late Mr. Arthur Morris of Leeds who invented this dance was not only a teacher of dancing but also an expert pianist. He was elected a member of the B.A.T.D. in 1897 and three years later he invented and composed the music of his now celebrated dance. He entered it in this annual competition held that year in the old St. James's Hall, London. The dance did not win; it did not even reach the final round, but Mr. David Day of Messrs. Francis, Day and Hunter, the music publishers, was so impressed with its possibilities that a meeting was arranged at his office the following day, and he agreed to publish it. It was felt, however, that the original routine was not quite satisfactory and Mr. Morris thought that it would be easier to pass from one movement to another if certain alterations were made. As the result, we had the Veleta as it is known today.

It was in the closing years of the century that we first hear of Blackpool as a dancing centre and the coming of those enormous popular ballrooms at the Tower and the Winter Gardens. Unfortunately, records do not appear to have been very carefully kept by either company. It does seem, however, that the Tower was opened on Whit Monday, May 14th, 1894, and the ballroom later on after reconstruction re-opened again in 1899. It was not for a number of years that dancing twice daily was held here. The Empress Ballroom at the Winter Garden seems to have been opened in 1896 and, for this occasion, there was a specially selected band of fifty performers from Covent Garden and other theatres who played dance music in the afternoon and evening under their conductor

Mr. Clarence C. Corri. The admission charge was 6d., and the programme consisted of a Grand March, Waltz, Schottische, Lancers, Polka and Quadrille. "Vocals" were apparently given by Mr. Alec Romar and Miss Margaret Radcliffe and the M.C. was a Mr. W. Dracup.

And so we have come to the end of our survey of Social Dancing in England during the nineteenth century. In these hundred years, though, of course, it was not realized at the time, we saw the birth of our modern dancing. Changes were going on all the time: new dances came, old dances went. But the most basic changes of all that the century witnessed were firstly the passing of the "Open-Couple" dance, such as the minuet, and the coming of the "Closed-Couple" dance, as exemplified in the waltz and the polka. And secondly, the turning to the New World, particularly the United States, for sources of inspirations for new dances and new rhythms.

# ★ 12 ★

## THE ORIGINAL STEPS AS DANCED

*A Description of the Correct Method of Waltzing*
by Thomas Wilson, London, 1816.

THE above is the oldest description in English which I have
of the early waltz. It was written about four years after the
dance in something approaching its modern form with the
close hold had made its appearance at Almack's as told on
page 63 of the present volume. Wilson's description of the
steps presupposes that these will be used in conjunction with
the arm movements as shown in the engraving reproduced
facing page 65. They do indicate, however, how our modern
waltz steps originated. I will confine my quotation to his description of the steps used in German waltzing and omit the
three variations of French waltzing.

> The following movements compose German Waltzing. The
> *left* Foot is passed into the *second position* on the *flat Foot*, fol-
> lowed by *two Coupées*, and made in the same place, one with
> each Foot; the *right* Foot passed forward into the *fourth position,*
> and the *left* Foot brought forward with a Rise or slight *Spring*
> into the *fifth position*, and immediately afterwards bringing the
> *right* Foot forward into the *fourth position.*
>
> *The Lady and Gentleman*, as in French Waltzing, make the
> same Movements in performing the German Waltz; but, as they

do not commence with the same Movement *together*, consequently the several Movements are not performed by *Lady* and *Gentleman* at the *same time*.

The *Gentleman* passes his *left* Foot into the *second position* and the *Lady* passes her *right* Foot into the *fourth position* forward.

Their situation is shewn by Fig. 3., with the *Exception*, that the feet of *both* should be placed *flatly*, instead of being *raised* on the *point*, as is there represented. [see plate facing page 65.]

The *Gentleman* afterwards makes a *Coupée* by bringing the *right* Foot *behind* the *left*, raising the *left* Foot a little; and immediately makes another *Coupée*, by placing the *left* Foot behind the *right* with a *slight spring;* but in a *close position*, and turning the Body at the *time* of *making* them.

The *Lady*, during the while the *Gentleman* is performing the *two Coupées*, passes her *left* Foot, (which is in the *fourth position behind*) with a *Rise* or slight *Spring* into the fifth position in *front*, and her *right* Foot is *immediately* afterwards brought into the *fourth position* in *front* again. And as the *Gentleman* passes his *right* Foot forward into the *fourth position* in *front* (which Movement succeeds the *second Coupée*, as before described); the *Lady* passes her *left* Foot into the *second position*, and proceeds to perform the *same Movements*, and in the *same Manner*, as described to be performed by the *Gentleman* (see Figure 9); and the *Gentleman* performs the *Movements* forward, and in the *same Manner*, as they are described to be performed by the *Lady*.

In continuing the Waltzing, the several Movements are performed in the order described, *alternately*, by *Lady* and *Gentleman*.

The above instructions have a footnote which will be read with considerable interest as the difficulty still arises today in what is known as the Old Time Waltz:

Such Persons as may have had but *little practice* in Dancing will experience so great a difficulty in bringing the Foot into the *fifth position*, as to prevent its being performed with apparent *ease,* the *third position* may therefore be substituted; and, if *passed* well into that position, will appear much more easy and pleasing to the observation, even of a *Professed Dancer,* than a *tolerable* attempt at passing the Foot into the *fifth position.*

---

De L'Art de la Danse
by J. H. Gourdoux-Daux, Paris, 1823.

Used by Carlo Blasis in his "Code of Terpsichore" (1830), and the following is taken from R. Barton's English translation of this work.

In the following quotation the sentences are very long and decidedly involved, but I have thought it better, as it is a quotation, to present it exactly as it originally appeared.

"It (the Waltz) is composed of two steps, each of three beats to a bar, which also contains three *tems,* according to musical principles. Each of these two steps performs the demi-tour, or half-turn of the waltz, which lasts during one bar; the two steps united form, therefore, the whole waltz, executed in two bars. These steps differ one from the other, yet so as to fit one into the other, if it may be so expressed, during their performance, and in such a manner as to prevent the feet of one from touching and endangering those of the other; thus while the gentleman performs one step, the lady dances the other, so that both are executed with uninterrupted exactness, as will be clearly demonstrated.

"In order to perform one of these waltz steps, place your feet in the third position, the right foot forward, then advancing the right foot in the natural way, not turning it out, to place it in the fourth position (first time); then immediately bring forward the left foot, turning the toe inward, and placing it crossways before the other foot, to form the fourth position, that foot being raised immediately, and the body is at the same time, turned half-round; in placing the foot for the fourth position (second time), that foot which you have raised, while placing the last mentioned, must then be placed before the other in the third position, and outwardly, resuming its ordinary posture, and to perform the third bar*. The step being thus executed while turning half round.

"In order to execute the second step, and to perform at the same time the other half-turn which completes the waltz, turn out the side of your left foot, the toe being inward, and moving the body round at the same time, place it in the second position, (first beat), put the right foot behind the left, always continuing to turn the body (second beat), then bring the left foot before you, turning the toe inwards, the body turning also, to come half round, at the moment you are placing the left foot in the second position, to execute the third beat of the second step, and the second half-turn, which completes the waltz.

"By this example, it may be seen that the waltz is composed of two steps, each of which contains three *tems*, or beats, making six for both, and for the entire figure of the waltz, which is performed during two bars; also, that when either of the two persons waltzing advances the right foot to begin the first step described above, the opposite person draws back the left foot at the same time to begin the other step, allowing his partner an opportunity of advancing her foot, both performing then the *demi-tour;* when one repeats the step the other has just executed in the second *demi-tour*, to complete the waltz. When the position for waltzing is taken, in order that the step may be properly commenced, and that both persons may be in unison, the lady being on the right of the gentleman, he must go off on the left foot, turning himself before his partner, as if that had been his first position, and with respect to the second step described before, it is always performed by that person who has his back towards the side on which the waltz begins, as the person who faces that side always executes the first step.

"To waltz properly, all the beats, or *tems*, should be clearly marked, being attentive not to turn upon the toes, in the same

---

* This would appear a wrong translation. The word should be beat, or time. It will be noticed Barton sometimes uses time and sometimes beat.

beats, such a system not being convenient for the turning of two persons at once; every turn in a waltz should be clearly and fully performed, so that on finishing, the waltzers should come always opposite to the same side as they were on setting out; without which, the course of the waltzes cannot be followed, and the waltzer would, in consequence, fall upon those who are coming behind him, or who are in the middle of the room, which is very frequently the case.

"Care should be taken not to make use of those vicious attitudes, the second of which is ever more indecent than the first, and which, indeed, have their origin in loose society.

"The gentleman should hold the lady by the right hand, and above the waist, or by both hands, if waltzing be difficult to her; or otherwise, it would be better for the gentleman to support the right hand of the lady by his left. The arms should be kept in a rounded position, which is the most graceful, preserving them without motion; and in this position one person should keep as far from the other as the arms will permit, so that neither may be incommoded."

---

*Fashionable Dancing*
by Cellarius, London, 1847.
Translated from the original French book *La Danse des Salons,* published in Paris in the same year.

"The gentleman should place himself directly opposite his lady, upright, but without stiffness; joining hands, the left arm of the gentleman should be rounded with the right arm of the lady, so as to form an arc of a circle, supple and elastic.

"The gentleman sets off with the left foot, the lady with the right.

"The step of the gentleman is made by passing the left foot before his lady. So much for the first time.

"He slides back the right foot, slightly crossed, behind the left,

An Evening at Windsor Castle

From a coloured lithograph of 1855 showing what appears to be a Double Set of Quadrilles in progress. Queen Victoria is partnered by the Emperor Napoleon III and the Prince Consort by the Empress Eugenie

GEORGE III BIRTHNIGHT BALL AT ST. JAMES'S PALACE

THE CAKE WALK

In the Southern States in the 80's the domestic staff were allowed to show their prowess before their master and his guests *(From "Down Memory Lane")*

the heel raised the toe to the ground. So much for the second time.

"Afterwards he turns upon his two feet on the toes, so as to bring the right foot forward, in the common third position; he then puts the right foot out, on the side, slides the left foot on the side, in turning on the right foot, and then brings the right foot forward, in the third position. So much for the fourth, fifth and sixth times.

"The lady commences, at the same moment as the gentleman, with the fourth time, executes the fifth and sixth, and continues with the first, second, and third; and so on.

"The preparation for this Waltz is made by the gentleman; he places the right foot a little in advance, on the first time of the measure, lets the second time pass by, and springs on the right foot, in readiness for the third time, and to set off with the first step of the waltz. This prelude serves as a signal for the lady.

"Before the first six steps are completed, they should accomplish an entire turn, and employ two measures of the time. Formerly they counted by three equal steps; this has been properly reformed, seeing that the first three steps are not made like the last. The best plan is, to count by six steps, connected one to the other, in order to make the pupil feel the time he should mark.

"In order to make my pupils understand how, by means of these six steps, a turn may be accomplished, I am accustomed, in my lessons, to place him opposite the wall. I then make him describe a half-turn with the three first steps, so that he finds his back turned against the wall; then to execute the last half-turn with the three other steps.

"The three first steps should contribute equally to the first half-turn; not so with the three last. At the fourth step, the gentleman should, without turning, place his foot between those of his lady, accomplish the half-turn, passing before the lady with the fifth step, and bring the right foot to its place with the sixth time.

---

## 2—THE VALSE À DEUX-TEMPS

*Fashionable Dancing*
by Cellarius, London, 1847.

Translated from the original French Book
*La Danse des Salons*, published in Paris in
the same year.

"The music of the Valse à Deux-Temps is rhythmed on the same measure as that of à trois temps, except that the orchestra should slightly quicken the movement, and accentuate it with special care.

"The step is very simple, indeed, is the same as that of the galop, executed by either leg while turning; only, instead of springing with this step, it must be carefully glided, avoiding leaps and jerks.

"I have already pointed out, in speaking of the valse à trois temps, the position of the foot. The knees should be slightly bent; when too rigid, they engender stiffness, and constrain to a leaping step; but this flexibility of the legs should not be too great—indeed, almost imperceptible. The waltzer should be himself sensible of it, rather than make it apparent to the eyes of the others; too great a bending is not only ungraceful, but is as injurious to the waltz as too great stiffness.

"A step must be made to each measure; that is, to glide with one foot, and *chasser* with the other. The valse à deux temps differing from the valse à trois, which describes a circle, is made on the square, and only turns upon the glissade. It is essential to note this difference of motion, in order to appreciate the characters of the two waltzes.

"The position of the gentleman is not the same in the valse à deux temps as in that à trois. He should not place himself opposite his lady, but a little to her right, and incline himself slightly with the right shoulder, so as to enable him to move easily in accordance with his partner.

"I have already expressed my regret at the title of à deux

temps being given to this waltz instead of à deux pas. The term à deux pas would have avoided much confusion, by indicating that two steps were executed to three beats of the music; the first step to the first beat, letting pass by the second beat, and executing the second step to the third beat. By this means we are sure to keep time with the measure.

"In the valse à deux temps, the gentleman begins with the left foot, the lady with the right.

"What I have stated, as to the attitude of the gentleman, applies partially to that of the lady. She also should avoid stiffness of the limbs, as well as of the arm, which is joined with that of the gentleman; and avoid leaning heavily on the shoulder or hand of her partner.

---

### 3.—POLKA.

*The Ballroom Polka, Polka Cotillon, and Valse à Deux Temps*
Arranged by M. Coulon. London, 1844.

1. There are but three times in the Polka, the fourth time being only a repose, to admit of preparation for the ensuing measures. The first time is marked by the gentleman beating slightly with the right foot, and by his sliding, almost simultaneously the left foot forward. During the second time he brings the right foot forward by a *glissade*; and at the third time, he advances a step with his left foot, and brings the right towards it, slightly bent backwards, and kept ready for the next measures. The lady starts with the right foot, and the gentleman with the left; in the meanwhile the gentleman holds his partner's left hand with his right.

2. Both advance *balançant*, right and left alternately, so as to find themselves one measure nearly *vis à vis*, and the other *dos à dos*. In doing this they must be careful to turn gracefully and not to indulge in any of those steps which border on theatrical dancing.

3. Both promenade in this position round the circle, the gentleman still retaining his hold of his partner's left hand, as
before.

4. After one, or several rounds, the gentleman releases the
lady's hand, to take her by the waist, as in the waltz.

5. They then perform *figures en avant* and *figures en tournant*,
alternately, always observing the characteristic cadence of
the Polka whose musical rhythm may be expressed as
follows:

*Illustrated London News*, May 11th, 1844.

### The Drawing Room Polka

La Polka, like its predecessors the waltz and galop, is a danse
à deux, couples following each other in the salle de danse, commencing at pleasure and adopting, of the following figures, that
which pleases them most at the moment. All those anxious to
shine at La Polka will dance the whole of them, returning from
time to time by way of rest, to the first figure.

Measure: 2/4, not so fast as a galop. Count 4.

Steps are two:

1st: (a) hop on r.f. lifting or doubling up l. at the same time.
    (b) l.f. boldly forward on the ground
    (c) r. toe to l. heel.
    (d) l.f. short step forward.

Repeat with alternate feet, proceeding in this step with arm
circling your partner's waist, round the room.

Change of figures left to gentleman.

2nd: same step, R. arm round partner's waist, but *backing* all
round the room, lady pursuing. Reverse.
In backing the leg, put boldly forward in 1st figure, is
now placed boldly back on the ground.

3rd: Same step, waltzing round room.

4th: Heel and toe.

5th: Back (reverse) waltz.

### Fashionable Dancing
by Cellarius, London, 1847.

The Polka is danced in *two-four-time*, a military march movement rather slow.

I will endeavour to give an idea of the step, begging my readers to excuse what in this demonstration, as in all others of the same kind, must be necessarily a little tedious; for in this, more than ever, I must put aside all pretension to elegance of style, and endeavour only to attain clearness and exactness.

The step of the Polka is divided into three times.

For the first time, the left heel must be raised to the side of the right leg, without passing behind it, and so as to glide along the calf. In this position you spring upon the right foot, so as to throw the left foot forward, which forms a *glissade en avant*.

The second and third times are composed of two *jetés*, or *petits pas sautés;* the first with the right, and the second with the left foot; taking care that the two feet are nearly on the same line.

At the second *petit pas*, you lift the right leg, the heel near to the lower part of the left calf; and you let the fourth time of the measure form a pause or rest, so that three times only are marked by the dance. You recommence with the glissade *en avant* of the right foot, and so continue alternately.

The gentleman should always begin with the left foot and the lady with the right, as in the ordinary waltz.

The polka presents in its execution many special evolutions, which contributed much to its variety, and which a practised dancer never fails thoroughly to acquire. He should cause his lady to turn in every way, to retire from or advance towards him in a right line, by means of that movement known to waltzers as the *redowa*; he should even, in certain cases, and when the crowd leaves to each couple scarcely space to move, *faire pivoter* his lady, in slackening his steps so as to form a space for himself.

## 4.—THE  QUADRILLE.

The Quadrille was introduced from Paris by Lady Jersey in 1815. The earliest printed description I have found is in an anonymous booklet entitled *Le Maître à Danser, or the Art of Dancing Quadrilles*, published in London in 1820. This claims to describe that set of Quadrilles generally known as "The First Set" and this is the one introduced by Lady Jersey at Almack's.

First Figure. LE PANTALON.
1. Chaîne Anglaise.
2. Balancez à vos dames.
3. Tour de Maine.
4. Chaîne des dames.
5. Demi Queue du chat.
6. Demi chaîne Anglaise.
      The same to be repeated by the six others.

Second Figure. L'ÉTÉ.
1. En avant deux de vis-à-vis.
2. En arrière.
3. Chassez and déchassez.
4. Traversez.
5. Chassez and déchassez.
6. Retraversez.
7. Balancez à vos dames.
8. Tour de main.
      The same to be repeated by the six others.

Third Figure. LE POULE.
1. Les deux de vis-à-vis, main droite and main gauche.
2. Balancez quatre sans vous quitter la main.
3. Demi Queue du chat.
4. En avant deux de vis-à-vis.
5. Dos-à-dos.
6. En avant **quatre.**
7. Demi chaîne Anglaise.
      The same to be repeated by the six others.

Fourth Figure. LA TRENIS.
1. Chaîne des dames.
2. Balancez à vos dames.
3. Tour de main.
4. A cavalier and his partner En avant and En arrière.
5. Idem En avant leading his partner to the left side of the cavalier opposite.
6. The two ladies cross over to the opposite place, while the cavalier crosses over between them.
7. The two ladies chassez-croisé, while the cavalier figure devant, and all come to their places as in No. 5.
8. The first lady went to the left of the cavalier opposite, makes a single balancé to her own partner and finishes with a Tour de main with him.
    The same to be repeated by the six others.

---

The following descriptions are taken from Blasis' Code of Terpsichore (1830) and he in his turn took them from *De L'Art de la Danse* by J. H. Gourdoux-Daux (1823). These are the fullest, and coincide with those given in a shorter form by Paine and the anonymous *Analysis of the London Ballroom*, and to some extent by Wilson and Desrat. The greatest divergence comes in the Final figure to which further reference will be made.

*The Figure called Le Pantalon or*

## CHAÎNE ANGLAISE.

1. The *chaîne Anglaise* is performed by two gentlemen and two ladies, opposite; they advance to change places and, in passing each other, they present the right hand; each gentleman after giving his right hand to the opposite lady who faces him, leaving her hand, he turns behind her, then gives his left to that of his partner, who is taking the place of the other lady; and all are again placed beside each other; each letting go hands

upon resuming their places. This figure, which is but the *demi-chaîne*, or half *chaîne Anglaise*, when repeated immediately on each resuming their places, is then called the *chaîne entière*, or whole *chaîne Anglaise*, as here performed; it requires the time of eight bars.

### BALANCE.

2.   Each gentleman and his partner turn towards each other and they set (balance) during four bars.

### UN TOUR DE DEUX MAINS.

3.   Immediately after having set, each couple take both hands, and turn round in their places; in regaining which, they leave go hands; this is performed in four bars.

## LA CHAÎNE DES DAMES.

4.   The two opposite ladies change places, and in passing give the right hand; afterwards they give the left hand to the two gentlemen who are remaining in their places. Each gentleman, immediately upon his partner's moving off to perform the *chaîne*, must go off to the right, at the same time presenting his left hand to the lady, who is entering the place of her partner; he must then turn upon his left to regain his place, where, having arrived, he leaves the hand of his partner. This figure, which is done during the time of four bars, is repeated also, to form the whole *chaîne*, which then requires eight bars, before each lady resumes her place.

### LA DEMI-QUEUE DU CHAT.

5.   Each person of two couple presents the left hand, and goes off obliquely to the right, in order to change places, on arriving at each other's place, they leave go hands: this requires four bars.

6.   To regain their places the two gentlemen and their partners perform the *demi-chaîne Anglaise* (see No. 1). The remaining couple do the same.

### The Figure called *L'Été*

1.  A gentleman and opposite lady advance and retire backwards, or *en avant deux*, during four bars.
2.  The same lady and gentleman cross and change places, passing from the right to the right, during four bars.
3.  The gentleman and the lady go off each on the right side and immediately return on the left, during four bars.
4.  The gentleman and lady re-crossing, regain their places, during the time of four bars.
5.  The gentleman then sets to his partner, and his partner to him. (See the Pantalon, No. 2.)
6.  Each couple makes the *tour de main*, as at No. 3 of the Pantalon, the remaining six doing the same.

In this figure called *l'Été*, after having performed the *en avant deux*, and gone off right and left, there is no more setting at the end. Custom alone has introduced the setting, which is intended only for that couple who have danced the figure among the rest; they then begin setting at the same time that the ladies of one couple, and the gentlemen of the other, commence crossing to regain their places, finishing equally at the same time, during four bars, after which follows the *tour de main*.

### The Figure called *La Poule.*

1.  The opposite lady and gentleman cross and give the right hand, during four bars.
2.  The same couple cross again, presenting then the left hand, which they continue to hold across the dance, remaining at the side during four bars.
3.  The gentleman and lady, still holding the left hand, now present each other the right, and set four in a-line, during four bars.
4.  The *demi-queue du chat* (see the Pantalon).
5.  The opposite gentleman and lady advance and retire backwards, during four bars.
6.  The same gentleman and lady then perform the *dos-à-dos*, turning round each other until they arrive at the place from

9*

which they set out; this requires four bars.

7.   Four advance and retire, similar to the *en avant deux.*

8.   The same four dance the *demi-chaîne Anglaise,* to regain their places (see the Pantalon). The remaining couple do the same.

### The Figure called Trenis.

1.   A gentleman and his partner present hands, then advance and retire twice, leaving hands at the second time; the lady going off, places herself to the left of the gentleman opposite, returns and retires backwards; this requires eight bars.

2.   A gentleman crosses between two ladies, being then in a line, and crossing at the same time right before them, they change with each other at the extremity, to make a repetition of the crossing together with the gentleman, and thus all three regain their places; this requires the space of eight bars.

3.   Set four (see Pantalon).

4.   Two gentlemen with their partners perform the tour de main (see Pantalon). The remaining couples do the same.

### The Figure called La Pastourelle (at first an alternative figure to La Trenis and subsequently more generally used).

1.   A gentleman and his partner present hands, then advance and retire twice, leaving hands at the second time; the lady then goes and places herself on the left of the opposite gentleman; which requires eight bars.

2.   The opposite gentleman, who is then between two ladies, gives a hand to each of them, and all three advance and retire twice, during eight bars.

3.   The remaining gentleman, who is left alone, then advances in his turn twice also, during eight bars.

4.   The same gentleman with the one opposite, and the two ladies by their side, advance and present hands to perform the hands half-round, until each is opposite to his own place, with his partner beside him: this is done in four bars.

5.   The same four do the half of *demi-chaîne Anglaise* to regain their places (see Pantalon). The remaining couple do the same.

### The Finale.

1. The two opposite gentlemen, each with his partner, perform a chassé-croisé; the gentleman dances a chassé while passing to the right, behind the lady, who at the same time performs a chassé on the left, while passing before him; afterwards they do the demi-balance, or half-setting, in the space of 4 bars.

2. The same two gentlemen and their partners perform the chassé-croisé back again; the gentleman on the left while re-passing behind his lady; and the lady on the right while re-passing before the gentleman; when regaining their places, they perform the demi-balance, or half-setting; during four bars.

3. En avant deux, or, opposite gentleman and lady (see figure of l'Été).

4. The same couple cross.

5. They then go off to the right and left.

6. The gentleman and lady re-cross to their places.

7. The two opposite gentlemen set to their partners (see Pantalon).

8. They then execute the tour de main.

9. The two ladies execute the chaîne.

10. The demi-queue de chat (see the above figure).

11. The half, or demi-chaîne Anglaise. The remaining six do the same; and to conclude, the whole eight dance the chassé, similar to the chassé-croisé of four (see preceding).

It should be noted that for some considerable time there were many different ways in which the final figure was danced. In one it will be remembered, about 1830, the Galop was introduced.

It is a little curious that, although in these early descriptions the dancers are instructed to ignore the first eight bars of each figure, there are no instructions for the bow or curtsy which comparatively modern dancers have introduced.

Coming down to the middle of the century, Cellarius in his

*Fashionable Dancing* published in 1847 has the following comments to make on the changes which the Quadrille had by that time undergone:

> I will confine myself to briefly stating the five figures which compose this quadrille, in order to point out the different changes or abbreviations which fashion has imposed.
>
> The first figure, ungracefully named Le Pantalon, is composed, as formerly, of right and left, balancez, ladies' chain, half promenade, and half right and left. The only change is the suppression of turning partners after balancez.
>
> The second figure, L'Été, is still composed of the avant-deux, the details of which are sufficiently known to all dancers. In this figure the turning partners after balancez is also suppressed.
>
> In the third figure, Le Poule, they no longer traverse on the right; they arrive slowly, giving the left hand to the opposite lady, the right hand to the partner, and wait the moment to balancez four in line. They have replaced the ancient dos-à-dos by two advance and retire twice, after which four advance and retire, then half right and left.
>
> In the fourth figure, named La Pastourelle, must be noted the suppression of the cavalier seul. It will be recollected that formerly, in this dance, this figure furnished to the cavalier an opportunity of displaying his talents. It may be easily conceived that this solo of the gentleman should have been suppressed, as it was not always exempt from a certain ridiculous pretension. Pastourelle is now executed with much less trouble; the gentleman conducts his lady to the opposite gentleman, who receives her with his left hand, and gives his right to his partner, taking care that the two ladies are placed slightly sideways; he then advances with them, retires, and again advances towards the opposite gentleman, who remains in his place; there he causes them to describe a half turn, and leaves them with the first gentleman, who executes with them the same figure that the other one has just performed.
>
> When the ladies turn the second time, they should find them-

selves so placed as to form a rond à quatre, followed by half right and left, which terminates the figure.

I need not speak of the figure called La Trenis, which was formerly performed instead of la Pastourelle. This figure, which is very well known, has ceased to be danced in the balls of distinction, and does not appear likely to regain its favour.

The fifth figure, called La Finale, requires no special observation; it is only a repetition of the avant-deux, preceded and followed by a chassé croisé à quatre, the three first times; the figure terminating by a general chassé croisé.

<hr>

### 5.—THE LANCERS.

The following description of Duval's Lancers, as danced at the Countess of Farnham's Ball at the Rotunda, Dublin, in 1817 (see page 70) is taken from a copy of the original music. This description is confirmed in a *Guide to the Ballroom* written by R. Hill and published in Lincoln in 1822.

1st fig. La Dorset. 1st Lady and opposite Gent. chassez to the right and left and swing quite round with right hand to place, 1st Lady and Gent, and opposite couple change places and back again, 1st Lady and Gent. passing in the centre and return to places passing outside, the 4 Gents join left hands in the centre at the same time, their right hands to their partners, all forming a cross and ballotez, the Gent. change places with their partners, the 4 Ladies coming to the centre, joining both right and left hands with each other, forming a cage, the 4 Ladies with hands joined dance round to the left, while the Gentlemen singly dance quite round the reverse way outside, then turn their partners to their places.

The other 6 do the same.

2nd fig. Lodoiska. 1st Gent and Lady advance and retire twice, the second time he leaves the Lady on the left of the opposite Gent. Chassez to the right and left and turn your partner right and left entirely. Balancez to the sides, then advance and retire in two lines, and turn partners to places.

The other 6 do the same.

3rd fig. La Native. 1st Lady chassez forward alone, then the opposite Gent. Both chassez to the right and pirouette chassez and glide together round to the left into their own places, then the four Ladies join their right hands in the centre, at the same time giving their left hands to their partner's left hand, all dancing quite round in the form of a cross, each Gent turns his partner round to the left into their own places.

The other 6 do the same.

4th fig. Les Grâces. One Gentleman and his partner with the Lady on his left, the three advance and retire twice, Balancez and pass between the two Ladies, three half round to the left and back again, the other three Gentlemen do the same figure, after which the Ladies do the same figure with the Gentlemen.

5th fig. Les Lanciers. Right and left all round making ballotez every time, the right and left hand is given, 1st Gent. gives his right hand to his partner's left, and turn half round in their own places, their backs to the 3rd couple, the 2nd Gent. and Lady follow the 1st couple, the 3rd Gent. and Lady follow the 2nd couple, the 4th Gent. and Lady follow the 3rd couple; only one couple advancing at a time, when all form in two lines, the Ladies on the right hand of the Gent. all facing the top of the room, then chassez all across twice, and pas de basque to the right, the Gent. turn off round to the left, and the Ladies to the Gent. following 1st Gent. and the Ladies following 1st Lady, when all are returned to the former situation they turn off, then form two lines, each Gent. facing his partner and chassez forward and back, each Gent. turns his partner into their own places.

Conclude with the grand square, viz. 1st & 3rd couple chassez forward, while the side couples chassez open; 1st & 3rd couple chassez open while the side couples chassez forward; 1st & 3rd couple chassez back, while the side couple chassez close; 1st & 3rd couple chassez into places while the side couples chassez backward into places. The figure commences next with the 2nd couple, then with the 3rd, then with the 4th, when the said couples commence the figure they chassez forward in the square while the 1st & 3rd couple chassez open.

The following description of Hart's Lancers is taken from *La Terpsichore Moderne*, a Ballroom Guide by J. S. Pollock. It appears to have been published about 1830. It will be noted that no names are given to the five figures.

1st. Opposite lady and gent. advance and set—turn with both hands, retiring to places—top couple lead between the opposite couple—return leading outside—set and turn at the corners.

2nd. First couple advance twice, leaving lady in the centre, set to partner in the centre—turn partners to places—all advance in two lines—all turn partner to places.

3rd. First lady advance and stop, then the opposite gentleman —both retire turning round—the ladies hands across quite round, at the same time, the gents lead round outside to the right, all resume partners and places.

4th. First couple set to couple at their right—set to couple at their left—change places with partners and set back again to places—right and left with opposite couple.

5th. Chain figure of eight half round, the same repeated to places, the first couple advance and turn facing the top, then the couple at right advance behind the top couple, then the couple at left and the opposite couple do the same, forming two lines, all change places and partners—back again—the ladies cast off to the right, while the gentlemen cast off to their left— meet and lead your partners up the centre—set in two lines, the ladies in one line, and gents. in the other—turn partners to places —(all promenade at the finish).

## 6.—CALEDONIANS.

The following description is taken from an early publication of the music.

### 1st Figure. Figure du Pantalon.

First and opposite couple, hands across and back again—Set and turn partners—Ladies chain—half promenade—half right and left—

### 2nd Figure. Figure de l'Été.

The first Gentleman advance twice and retire—the four Ladies set to the Gentlemen at their right, and turn with both hands, each taking the next Ladies place—all promenade.

### 3rd. Figure. Figure de La Poule.

Lady and opposite Gent; advance and retire—back to back—top couple lead between the opposites, return leading outside —set at the corners, and turn with both hands to places—all round.

### 4th Figure. Figure de la Pastourelle.

First Lady and opposite Gent. advance, and step, then their partners advance—turn partners to places—the four Ladies move to the right into next Ladies Place and stop—the 4 Gents; move to the left, into next Gents. place and stop—Ladies repeat the same to right—Gents. repeat the same to left—all join hands and lead round to places—all turn partners.

### 5th Figure. Figure de La Grand Finale.

First Gentleman lead his partner round, inside the figure— the 4 ladies advance join right hands, and retire—then the Gents. do the same—all set and turn partners—all chain figure half round—promenade to places—all change sides, join right hands, at corners and set—back again to places—(all promenade at the finale).

## 7.—THE BARN DANCE.

As described by the late Major Cecil Taylor:

### Steps for the Gentleman.

Glide left foot forward (1), close right foot behind left foot (2), glide left foot forward (3), bring right foot forward, raised from the floor and hop lightly on the left foot (4). Repeat, commencing on right foot. The Lady performs the same steps on the opposite feet.

Face partners and hold as in the Waltz and make two complete turns of the Waltz, counting 1 and 2-3 and 4-1 and 2, 3 and 4. The steps described in à trois temps being used.

---

## 8.—THE WASHINGTON POST.

The following description by Mr. William Lamb coincides with my personal memory of this dance:

### (Six-eight tempo)

Position.—The gentleman stands behind the lady with his right shoulder level with her right shoulder, both hands joined above the lady's shoulders, right hand to right, left hand to left hand. Both commence with right foot.

### First Part (Four Bars).

First Step—Spring upwards from both feet and alight on the left foot (toes), with the right foot pointed in the second position. Second Step—Spring upwards from the left foot, and simultaneously bring the right behind the left (one bar). **Again spring on the left foot and point the right in second position, then with** another slight spring on the left, pass the right foot in front of left (one bar). Repeat the four steps, commencing with the left foot (two bars).

### Second Part (Four Bars).

Take four long galop slides obliquely forward with the right foot (two bars). Repeat with left foot (two bars).

# INDEX